FROM THE
BLUE WINDOWS

Recollections of life in Queenstown, Singapore,
in the 1960s and 1970s

Tan Kok Yang

Home is a name, a word, it is a strong one; stronger than the magician ever spoke, or spirit ever answered to, in the strongest conjuration.

- CHARLES DICKENS (1812 –70)

饮水思原

To forget one's ancestors is to be a brook without a source, a tree without roots.

- CHINESE PROVERB

Published by:

Ridge Books
an imprint of NUS Press
National University of Singapore
AS3-01-02, 3 Arts Link
Singapore 117569

Fax: (65) 6774-0652
E-mail: nusbooks@nus.edu.sg
Website: http://www.nus.edu.sg/nuspress

ISBN: 978-9971-69-650-4 (paper)

National Library Board, Singapore Cataloguing-in-Publication Data

Tan, Kok Yang.
    From the blue windows : recollections of life in Queenstown, Singapore, in the 1960s and 1970s Tan Kok Yang. – Singapore : Ridge Books an imprint of NUS Press, c2013.
    p. cm.
    ISBN: 978-9971-69-650-4 (pbk.)

    1. Queenstown (Singapore) -- History 2. Queenstown (Singapore) -- Guidebooks 3. Singapore -- Social life and customs -- 20th century. I. Title.

    DS609.9
    959.57 -- dc23   OCN828626020
    Cover Illustration by: Koh Hong Teng
    Photographs by: Tan Kok Yang
    Typeset by: Md Faizal, SC (Sang Choy) International Pte Ltd
    Printed by: Mainland Press Pte Ltd

Published with the Support of

NATIONAL ARTS COUNCIL
SINGAPORE

Dedicated to the memories of
my beloved grandmother, Quek Wu Teck;
my father, Tan Han Kiat and
my mother, Lim Hui Noi

ACKNOWLEDGEMENTS

I would like to express my thanks and gratitude to the following establishments and persons for their support of this book:

The National Arts Council of Singapore (NAC), for awarding me the publishing grant, and Li Sihui, for her guidance on the grant application procedure.

NUS Press, especially Paul H. Kratoska, Publishing Director, for agreeing to publish this book, and Christine Chong and Riya de los Reyes, for editing the book and providing the necessary marketing assistance respectively.

My PhD supervisor, Anthony Sorensen (UNE, Armidale Australia) for writing the Foreward; and for reading and commenting on early manuscripts, Low Guat Tin (NIE), my secondary school English teacher, and Lau Kim Teng (NUS), my former Physics teacher in Secondary Four.

Two individuals at NUSS also went the extra mile when I was writing this book. On top of reading drafts, Lai Kim Seng suggested I write about the *pasar malam* of yesteryear while Johnny Tan, the ex-President of NUSS, gave me ideas on how to promote the book.

Clearly, all my siblings and Small Aunt have been invaluable in shaping this book; after all, they shared many of my memories at Queenstown. In particular, my younger brother, Kok Siang (NIE), fact-checked the events related to our family; while my two younger sisters, Joyce and

Alice, were very supportive during the process of writing. I must thank Joyce for reading the first manuscript. I would like to also thank Small Aunt for the love she has given me, and for contributing the many precious old black and white photographs to the book.

I wish to thank the love of my life, my wife, Lee Boon, for her love, support, and encouragement. A Teochew like myself, Lee Boon was a great help to me in the presentation of many points regarding our customs and tradition as well as in some of the Chinese translations. Our two wonderful young adult children, Toh Liang and Amanda, have provided me with the motivation and drive to write this book for them. Hopefully, they will have a better understanding of what life was like in the 1960s and 1970s in Queenstown.

This book would not be possible without the supporting work and contribution of many other individuals whose names are not mentioned above and I wish to thank them all.

FOREWORD

FROM THE BLUE WINDOWS

It was simultaneously a surprise, honour, and privilege that my friend and former doctoral student Tan Kok Yang invited me to write this introduction to his reminiscences of growing up in Singapore's Queenstown estate during the 1960s and 1970s. It was a pleasant surprise when a draft copy of *From the Blue Windows* emerged unheralded from my inbox about a year ago. At the time I had no idea of its existence and long gestation, but I had often wondered about Kok Yang's family background. My curiosity arose naturally during my many visits to Singapore during the 1990s when I sometimes stayed in his house with him and his family.

From the Blue Windows delighted me in many ways. On the surface it documents childhood memories of life in a large family living in often cramped conditions, local friendships and ties within a multi-cultural community, episodes of hardship and sadness, the daily grind of working life, changing environmental conditions, and the provision of community and personal services. Kok Yang weaves these dimensions into a rich chronological tapestry and set me thinking about my early post-war upbringing in England — so much so that I am trying to emulate the author's approach to document my own formative years for my family and posterity.

One of the perhaps unintended charms of this book is the likelihood that it will trigger a similar response in others. Below the surface, however, I found yet another story — a parable of Singapore's emergence as a nation. Kok Yang documents with vigour and colour many of the drivers of Singapore's success: ambition and drive, hard work, thrift, understanding and tolerance between populations from different ethnic backgrounds, and compassion for the less well-off. Tan Kok Yang, as a successful professional working in the field of Acoustics, is a typical product of this culture. I admired his drive as a student and his subsequent professional achievements. Thus, in a way, *From the Blue Windows* is a personal guide to self-improvement.

It was therefore a privilege for me to be among the first to read it and I look forward to adding the final version to my library. Indeed, I was deeply honoured to write this introduction to the book. It is testimony to our mutual regard, to international friendship, and to the universal importance of the strong values and behaviours so evident in *From the Blue Windows* in bringing about peace and prosperity.

Tony Sorensen
Adjunct Professor
University of New England, Armidale, Australia
26 September 2012

PREFACE

FROM THE BLUE WINDOWS is a first-hand account of events based on my recollections while growing up in the public housing estate in Queenstown, Singapore. This area was then known colloquially as "The Blue Windows" because of the unique, blue Georgian-wired glass louvred windows in the low-rise housing estate. Being one of the earliest public housing estates in Singapore, Queenstown has since undergone immense changes and celebrated its 60th anniversary in 2012.

I wrote this book over a period of ten years out of a love for the Blue Windows. This is how common people once lived in one of the first housing estates in Singapore. In the book, I have tried to recount nostalgically the times and lives in Queenstown during those early days. Indeed, I hope that this book will bring back fond memories of times past, and successfully evoke the lives of the people who once lived there. The episodes in *Blue Windows* cover the period from when I was an inquisitive seven-year-old boy to my teenage years, when a redevelopment programme in the estate forced my family to move to Tiong Bahru. For me, the memories of my early childhood are inseparable from the joy of the festive seasons, and other interesting occurrences at the Blue Windows. As such, I have intentionally filled the book with what I hope are fascinating recollections of the customs, lifestyle, and games that we played as children during those days.

I have also included poignant real-life stories of people who resided at the Blue Windows — some were relatives, others were neighbours and the rest were technically strangers — and hope that they that may give readers a better understanding of the socio-economic situation of Singaporeans at that time. Although this work is neither political nor academic, I have also touched on historical events in Singapore's past — such as the racial riots and the student unrest in the 1960s — from the perspective of how they impacted the daily lives of residents at the Blue Windows.

Indeed, the mention of the Blue Windows invokes memories of the simple, yet fulfilling lifestyle of Queenstown residents during the 1960s and 1970s. Through the narrative, it is my wish that readers take away an understanding of the humble, "kampung-like" lifestyle then. Unfortunately, such a way of life no longer exists in modern-day Singapore. I hope that this modest work will appeal to anyone with an interest in Singapore's past and the various districts that have a rich history. Hopefully, the tales in this book can also offer readers, particularly those from the younger generation, a glimpse of what life was like in Queenstown in the not-too-distant past. Perhaps it will enable readers to have a better understanding of our roots here in Singapore, and help them appreciate the richness of the multi-cultural and multi-racial way of life in Singapore.

The tales and happenings in this book are now but precious memories. Yet this book will allow the experiences I had living at the Blue Windows to be recorded for posterity. I believe that those who have at one time or another experienced living there, will from time to time fondly recall those good old days at the Blue Windows. This is my tribute to my family, old neighbours and friends, any fortunate ones who share a connection with Queenstown, especially those who lived there, and to Queenstown itself.

The stories and tales in this book are based on the author's experiences during the early part of his life living in Queenstown, Singapore till the early 1970s.

Almost all the characters and persons named in this book are actual names and nicknames known to the author. Some have been changed to protect the privacy of the persons involved and their families.

CONTENTS

1. EVERYDAY LIFE AT THE BLUE WINDOWS

My early years 01

Our government rental flats 02

Around Margaret Drive 05

The small hill at Stirling Road 08

Forfar House and Princess House 10

After sunset 14

The wet market 18

Hawkers 21

The old farmer 27

The neighbourhood shops 28

Tah Chung Emporium 30

The barber 31

The "dentist" 32

2. INSIDE THE HOUSE

Home décor 35

Salt refrigerators, charcoal stoves and a stone rice grinder...... 36

The bathroom 38

Our sleeping arrangements 39

Our first home telephone 40

Rediffusion Singapore and the gramophone 41

Television sets and RTS 41
Early cameras and typewriters 45
Wrist watches, school bags and fountain pens 47

3. FAMILY, FRIENDS AND NEIGHBOURS

Our clothes 49
Dialects and Singlish 52
Cars of the 1970s 54
A failed romance 56
My "aunty" and godparents 57
A tab at Ng Kee 59
The kampung spirit 60
Good and bad neighbours 61
Work 63

4. SCHOOL DAYS IN THE 60S AND 70S

Strathmore Primary School 69
A regular day at school 71
Significant primary school events 72
Faring badly in primary school 74
Jervois West Primary School 77
Kim Seng Technical School 80
Our hobbies 82
My pen pal 87
The GCE 'O' level examination 92
The National Cash Registers (NCR) and the F&N factory 93

5. CUSTOMS AND FESTIVALS

"Red" and "white" occasions 95
Chinese New Year 97

Tomb Sweeping Festival 105
Dragon Boat Festival 107
Hungry Ghost Festival 108
Double Seventh Festival 113
Mid-autumn festival 115
Christmas 118
A newborn in the family 121
"Stepping out of the Garden" Ceremony 123
Chinese weddings.. 124
Malay weddings 127
Birthday celebrations 128
Funerals 129

6. MEMORABLE EVENTS

A neighbour's eviction 135
Flash floods and blackouts 136
The Bukit Ho Swee fire 138
Chinese school students' demonstration 139
Racial riots 141
Student activists at Nanyang University 143

7. A NEW QUEENSTOWN

Rumours of redevelopment 145
A more modern lifestyle 146
Changing family circumstances 147
Moving house 148
Tiong Bahru 149

AFTERWORD 152
MAP... 156

CHAPTER 1

GROWING UP AT THE BLUE WINDOWS

My Early Years

I was born in the mid-1950s at the then Kandang Kerbau (KK) Hospital near Serangoon Road and spent the first year of my life in a cramped room that my parents rented along River Valley Road. The fourth child in my family, I was a quiet baby. My parents told me that I was indifferent to stimuli and did not even cry when I was hungry. They were apprehensive about the state of my body and my mind. Modern day doctors might have diagnosed me as having autism but I doubt my parents even knew of this term at that time.

Perhaps my passivity was due to the circumstances I was born into. My younger sister came to this world a year after I was born. As she was born with a severe medical condition, the new baby required more attention than I did. Perhaps I felt it was pointless to cry even when there was a real need on my part since my parents had to pay more attention to my physically weaker baby sister. Her condition also required regular medical treatment at the then St Andrew Mission Hospital downtown, and later at the then Outram Road General Hospital (now Singapore General Hospital). My paternal grandmother from China, whom we called "Ah mah" in Teochew, seemed to be the only one in the family who doted on me — the boy neglected but not unloved by his parents. Besides, it was also very common during those days, perhaps even now, for the Chinese to value boys more than girls (重男轻女).

As a small boy, I was rather quiet and unassuming. Fortunately, or unfortunately, I turned out otherwise as the years went by. According to my parents, I gradually became very active, if not downright mischievous. My hyperactive behavior caused them much dismay. Besides, I was extremely weak in my studies, which added to my woes as a child. My other siblings performed much better than me, so much so that my father practically gave up on my doing well at school.

I was told that my family initially stayed in a row of shophouses along River Valley Road. I was too young to recall exactly what happened when a fire destroyed that home together with a number of other houses. By the time I came to be more aware of my surroundings, the family had moved to a new government housing estate called Queenstown.

Our government rental flats

My family moved to Margaret Drive after that fateful fire. That cluster of three- and four-storey flats were neatly arranged in square configurations. In Queenstown, many of the three-storey low-cost flats were installed with typical blue-glass louvred windows. The people who lived there called their estate the "Blue Windows"; "*Lam Poh Lay*" in Hokkien (蓝玻璃, blue glass) and "*Nam Tieng Meng*" in Teochew (蓝天门, "blue sky doors"). It was not uncommon that someone who wished to go to Queenstown to visit friends and relatives would tell the taxi driver to go to the Blue Windows. Those flats with blue glass were unique

The signature blue-glass windows that gave the estate its informal name

— one could not find flats with such signature windows anywhere else in Singapore.

My parents lived with my grandmother, an aunt and eight children in an 800 square feet, rented first-floor apartment at Block 94 along Margaret Drive Road. During the 1960s and 1970s, it was common for extended families with at least three generations to live together under one roof. It was very unlike our present-day nuclear families where married couples only stay with their children and sometimes, a live-in domestic helper. Ours was a typical example of such large families who lived together.

The layout of our flat was simple yet functional. A big extended family like ours, we had to be content with two bedrooms and a bathroom cum toilet. My parents and sisters shared one room and my grandmother and my father's sister, whom we called Small Aunt (小姑), took the other. The kitchen was a decent size and is comparable

Three-storey flats near my block along Margaret Drive in the late 1970s, built by the Singapore Improvement Trust (SIT).

to our modern-day kitchen. The same cannot be said for the living room, which was also our dining room and the make-shift bedroom for my two older brothers and me at night. Because of space constraint, we boys had to sleep on folded green canvas beds in the hall.

Despite its small size, our flat had the luxury of a size-able balcony in front of the living room. It was here that Grandma took care of her favourite plants, one of which was a beautiful Christmas pine tree in a pot. Till today, I still remember how I would admire the leaves of this amazing tree in our little garden and feel a sense of happiness each time. Grandma was surely even more pleased than me as she was very proud of her tiny garden. That balcony was also a hideout for us kids and we used to play and hang around there for all our boyish activities. Once, my elder brother even kept a homemade concrete fish tank there. We also set off our firecrackers during the Chinese New Year there. People

Low-rise two-storey terrace houses built by SIT at the Dawson Estate. These have been torn down but similar units still stand along Stirling Road.

were allowed to light firecrackers for many years before it was banned. Fortunately, there was not a single incident of misfire or injury among us.

Our daily lives were routine. Father would go to work as a cashier at the then Sime Darby at the Robinson Road area very early in the morning while Mother prepared breakfast for us before we headed to school. Grandma, together with Small Aunt, would help with the household chores and look after my younger siblings. Life was not rosy in terms of material comfort or luxury, but we lived our days simply, humbly, and for the most part contentedly.

Around Margaret Drive

Life moved slowly and quietly for families at the Blue Windows. Our home was quite well-positioned, with the back of the flats facing three primary schools that were

Children playing badminton at the badminton court in front of our three-storey flat, Block 94 in the 1960s. This was the only badminton court in the area and served as a multi-purpose gathering point for the community. (Photo by the author's father.)

parallel to each other. The front of our house faced an open field with a badminton court in the centre. This court was a vital part of the landscape where we lived, acting as a gathering place for residents during both happy occasions such as weddings or birthday parties, and sad ones, such as funeral wakes. This meant that the first thing on everyone's mind when a lorry drove up to the badminton court was this: was there going to be a happy or sad event? To reduce the sense of unease, families put up a red cloth banner on the make-shift tent as soon as possible. Of course, the residents also used the badminton court to play a simple game of badminton in the evening after work. At such times, the court would be lit up on both sides with electricity tapped from the flat of one of the players. No public lighting for the court was available then.

The view from the balcony of our first floor flat at Block 94, Margaret Drive. Below the tree, in between the two blocks of flats was the "green bridge" that spanned Alexandra canal.

Next to our flat was Alexandra canal. The big canal, which was then also famously known as the "Boh Beh Kang" (Hokkien: 无尾港, "no tail river"), was the origin of the Singapore River and its water flowed southeast to the Singapore River and northwest upstream to Sungei Pandan or Pandan River. The canal passing through our little neighbourhood had two small bridges across it. During the early 60s, bridges were constructed entirely of timber planks, and would rot to such an extent that they would squeak and shake when we walked on them! The canal would often overflow during the rainy season. Sadly, there were incidences of young children falling through the bridges into the knee-deep muddy water, sometimes with grave consequences but mostly with slight injuries.

The white concrete pedestrian bridge that led to Princess Estate in 1996. Strathmore Primary School stands in the background. The canal was subsequently filled in with concrete.

The small hill at Stirling Road

In those days, families used to visit one another during their free time, especially during weekends and public holidays. After all, there was no television or other forms of entertainment to occupy oneself with after work. Visits to neighbours' houses were called "*kuah ke*" (Teochew: 过家, "crossing house"). My grandmother and father loved visiting, while my mother, a more private person, did not like it quite as much.

My grandmother's good friend, "Lau Gou" (Teochew: 老姑, old aunt) and her family, lived quite near to us, at the foot of a small hill, where the current Stirling estate now stands. She was caring, hardworking and a very like-able person who worked part-time for my family as a laundry woman and helped my mother with some household chores. In the mid-60s, Grandma would bring along

The "green bridge" that led to the wet market along Strathmore Avenue in 1996. The canal was subsequently filled in with concrete.

a few of her grandchildren when she visited Lau Gou. Interestingly, Grandma would always insist that I put on an improvised hat, made by tying knots on all four corners of a cotton handkerchief, during these visits. Despite the fact that Grandma never left home without her waxed paper umbrella, this served as extra protection from the sun.

On the way up the hill, probably what is now called Mei Ling Heights, there were a number of Hokkien and Teochew families living in timber houses with *attap* roofs. This kampung was named after Boh Beh Kang, and its residents were mostly farmers who raised poultry and some pigs. Some of the produce was sold at the nearby wet markets and the rest were kept for self-consumption. Because of the abundant vegetation and the presence of water streams, the residents there also planted a variety of vegetables and fruit trees. Durian and rambutan trees were abundant on the hill sides. However, the dirt paths leading up the hill got slippery and uneven during rainy seasons. Besides, the pungent odour of poultry and pig waste, coupled with some old graveyards along the way up the hill, made a trip up the hill unattractive, especially for schoolchildren like me.

That small hill at Stirling Road evokes many memories, one of which is the sweet aroma of freshly baked bread. We went to the government polyclinic at the top of the hill whenever we fell sick. Next to this small and simple clinic was a bakery. Even before we reached the clinic, we could smell the aroma of bread. To this day, the sight and smell of any bakery reminds me of my numerous child-hood visits to the polyclinic with my grandmother. During those days, when a child in the family fell ill, the casual way of life then meant it was quite common for one or more to follow suit. And so, once a trip was made to the clinic, a few other trips tended to follow soon after.

As children who were brought up in a traditional Chinese family, we listened to Grandma's instructions obediently. Father was always at work from early morning to late evening and Mother was always busy with house-work. That left Grandma to help look after the young children in the family. Nevertheless, given the simple lifestyle of yesteryear, bringing up children was never as demanding as it is nowadays. Comparing my childhood to my childrens', mine seemed far more enriching and exciting despite the lack of material comfort back then.

Forfar House and Princess House

To reach the top of the small hill, we had to pass by a majestic brick building: the Forfar House at Princess Estate. Forfar House, which has since been demolished, was known

Forfar House in 1996. It was subsequently demolished; Forfar Heights now stands in its place.

to the locals as "Chap Si Lau" (Hokkien: 十四楼, fourteen storeys) as it was the only fourteen-storey building at that time and was once the tallest residential building in Singapore.

A secondary school classmate of mine, Lee Eng, stayed on the fourth floor of Forfar House. I used to visit him after school to discuss our homework and pass the time by loitering around the neighbourhood together. Being one of the very few high-rise buildings in the early 60s, it was not surprising that there were cases of people taking their lives by jumping down from one of the open corridors on the higher floors. As a young boy, I did not understand what suicide meant; we were simply told to avoid going near Forfar House, especially at night. Moreover, in the 1960s and 1970s, street lights were few and far between. This gave the place an even more eerie atmosphere after sunset.

11

My grandmother scared my siblings and I into submission by telling us about *pontianaks*, spirits of women who had died while pregnant. They hung themselves off old trees with overhanging branches, she said, and had long, bloody tongues. According to Grandma, they specifically targeted naughty children who did not listen to their parents or teachers, and would try to suck blood off them if they passed by. After hearing that story repeated to us, it soon became hard to get us to step out of the flat alone after dark. Another place that evoked fear in us was the Queenstown Remand Prison, just behind the Queenstown Library. It was a dark, deserted area and was also said to be haunted.

However, I felt safe if an adult accompanied me. On many occasions, usually in the evening or over the weekend, I followed my father to his journalist friend's house. He was staying in one of the seven-storey flats next to Forfar House. I recall my father's friend being a rather serious person while his wife was a very kind and friendly woman. They had three children. One of their sons was a school teacher while their daughter worked as a nurse at the Outram Road General Hospital. Their eldest son was mentally disabled. During those visits to their three-room flat, I was quite scared of the strange-looking man. He would be squatting on the floor, using his palm to tap the bare concrete flooring lightly and repeatedly. Father assured me that he was harmless; explaining simply that the man was mentally disabled and that his parents had to look after him as though he were still a child. Father also reminded me to be kind to people like him. That was indeed an early lesson in compassion that I continue to bear in mind today. At that time, there were no communal institutions that looked after persons like him. As fate

A block of seven-storey SIT flats where many of Father's friends stayed in the 1960s and 1970s.

would have it, the man's father eventually died of lung cancer. After his friend's demise, friendship and compassion prompted my father to devote a lot of his free time to visiting his friend's son and giving him and his family moral support. Fortunately, they did not face any financial difficulty because the other children were already working adults.

Next to the Forfar House stood Princess House, the headquarters of the then Singapore Improvement Trust (SIT), the equivalent of the present-day Housing and Development Board (HDB). Its red brick walls gave it a dignified and official look. That building housed the government officials and it was also there that my parents went to pay the rent for our flat, a mere 50 dollars a month. Fortunately, this iconic landmark was set aside for conservation in 2007.

Princess House in the 1960s, where the Singapore Improvement Trust (SIT) was located.

After sunset

Working at the then Sime Darby as a cashier meant that my father returned home at only seven or eight in the evening. We hardly had dinner with him. Instead, we usually ate with Mother, Grandma and Small Aunt. After dinner, Grandma would bring us children to the ground floor and spread a straw mattress on the badminton court for all of us to sit on. At times, other older neighbours would join her to chit-chat. Meanwhile, we children would play tag, known colloquially as "catching". As the sun set, we gave the court up to a group of working uncles to play badminton. My father joined in occasionally for such games, but eventually pulled out of the group because of the demands of work.

Sometimes after dinner, my parents would take evening walks with us children. Our usual route would be to the then Queenstown Secondary Technical School and back to our flat at Margaret Drive. There were few cars or buses along Dawson Road then and such evening walks were very leisurely pursuits. On many occasions in the early 1960s, we even encountered herds of cows crossing our path. These cows were taken care of by an elderly Indian man who would sell their milk for a living. For a few cents, residents could order milk from him and he would place a bottle of milk at your doorway every evening or morning. Somehow, the cows suddenly stopped appearing when the Stirling Road hill started to be developed into a new public high-rise estate. I missed the cows badly as a boy but was also afraid of them and did not like the smell of cow droppings.

At night, the entire neighbourhood was lit dimly by the few street lights that existed at that time. Unlike our modern day sodium lamps, these mercury lamps gave off a faint bluish-white light. Night time in our estate was generally a time of peace and solitude. The air there was also very fresh, mainly because the estate consisted of low rise, two to three-storey buildings. Admittedly, there was not much of a view, but there was no shortage of greenery. Like my grandmother's little garden, which she looked after so fervently in the balcony of our flat, many residents who lived on the ground floor had humble little gardens in their front or backyard.

After nine o'clock, there were not many people on the streets, in the badminton court, or in the open field. There was hardly any nightlife during those days, except for special festivals such as the Seventh Lunar Month or Chinese New Year. We would, however, have a *pasar malam* (Malay: night market) once a month. It was held along the narrow Margaret Drive, near the Queenstown Library. Unlike our present day *pasar malam*, all the stalls made use of kerosene lamps. Clearly, most of the stuff that hawkers

15

sold then was quite different from what is sold nowadays. During those days, there was no high-tech equipment like mobile phones, computer games, or electronic goods, and most stalls sold clothing, bed sheets, kitchen wares, utensils, stationery and so on.

Despite the dimly lit neighbourhood, there were not many serious crimes, although we heard of the usual gang fights from time to time. However, pickpocketing did occur sometimes. I myself fell victim to a young hooligan when I was walking home after visiting a friend across the canal. This guy, hardly a real adult gangster, accosted me while I was crossing the green bridge and put his hand on my shoulder. He claimed that he knew me and was an old friend, which was anything but true. As a young school boy, I was very frightened and knew very well that he was up to no good. True enough, he took my small wallet from my shirt pocket forcefully and ran away as fast as he could. Shocked and traumatized, I rushed back home and related the incident to my mother. Small Aunt was particularly sympathetic towards me and immediately started a little donation drive among my family members to make up for my loss. In the end, I managed to recoup the few cents that were taken from me. I was deeply grateful to Small Aunt and my siblings. Still, I was too scared to go out on my own for many days after that incident.

During my secondary school days, I used to do my homework with my older brothers at the balcony of our tiny flat in the evening after dinner. Grandma and my parents would watch television programmes in the living room while we revised our homework. They always turned down the volume of the television set so as not to disturb us. Nevertheless, we could still hear the music and songs from traditional Teochew drama and Chinese variety shows. However, we got so used to studying and hearing all the noise at the same time that there was really no cause for complaint. From our balcony, we also could hear a pushcart hawker, who sold Teochew fried *kway teow* at the corner of the opposite block of flats, frying noodles on his wok. In a way, it never occurred to us that all this noise could be annoying; strange as it seems, these sounds gave our estate a soothing aural backdrop that we grew accustomed to.

The uncle selling fried *kway teow* was not the only night-time hawker in the area. I remember another hawker who sold homemade bread across the canal at the end of the green bridge. The store was manned by a petite middle-aged widow whose husband had died in a shipyard accident. She had to resort to working as a hawker to support her young children and mother-in-law. When I felt hungry after a long night of doing homework, I used to walk a short distance from my flat to buy bread from this aunty. I can still recall her tired demeanour — unsurprising, given her unfortunate circumstances — but she was always kind and helpful to her customers.

From the balcony of our flat, I could see the dim light of the distant kerosene lamps where both hawkers worked late into the night. Even as a secondary school boy, watching them from afar inspired me; I could not help admiring their hard work. Their relentless effort to provide for their families reinforced my determination to study hard in order to be able to support my parents once I started working. The lighted stores amidst the darkness and silence of the Blue Windows set a rather special feeling of homeliness and love. I continue to miss that serenity and often wonder if I will be able to witness such a scene in our heartlands again.

Strathmore Avenue in the 1990s. Except for the parking sign (right), this area looked almost exactly the same as it did when I walked along here in the 1970s on the way to the wet market.

The wet market

As a small boy, I used to accompany my mother to the wet market, which was a short walk from our flat. It was an interesting place for me. The market place, which was near to Princess House, was usually crowded as it was the only wet market around the Blue Windows.

Those days, each housewife would carry a cane basket to the market to pick up their foodstuff. Waxed paper umbrellas and squarish paper bags printed with Chinese words were also a common sight at the Blue Windows. Plastic umbrellas or bags were unheard of in those days. Grandma would always tuck a waxed paper umbrella under her arm when she went out to visit neighbours or when she went to the market. She also used a squarish paper bag to hold rice flour. Although the food available was basically similar to what we have

The wet market and food center, along Strathmore Avenue and in front of Princess House. They have since been demolished.

now, things were done more simply then. Fish, meat, and vegetables were wrapped with used newspapers. Indeed, it was much more environmentally friendly than it is now.

Of course, none of today's "high-tech" foods were available then. Things like mass-produced fish balls and genetically modified fruits were unheard of. Instead of electronic weighing machines, hawkers used *daching*, or rudimentary wooden beam balances with a central pivot and two scales, to weigh the fish, meat or other food stuffs. Lacking the luxury of the modern calculator, they used the Chinese abacus to work out the total price chargeable. During those days, plastic bags and containers for cooked food were unheard of. The hawkers made do with banana or *opeh* (Malay [?]: *upih*, betel nut palm) leaves. The *opeh* leaf, light-brown in colour, is less commonly used today. However, it seems like Hainanese fried *kway teow* tasted better on *opeh*

19

A typical pushcart hawker in the mid-1960s. They used charcoal stoves for cooking, and opeh leaves for wrapping food. (Reproduced with permission from Mr. Ong, owner of Yong Kee Chai Tau Kway, Bukit Timah 7 Mile Market Hawker Centre.)

than it does on the sheet of plastic or waxed paper that we use now.

I sometimes went to the market alone to run errands for my parents. The hawker whom my mother used to buy bean sprouts from was also an illegal bookie who took bets for a very popular game at that time in the 60s, known as "*chap ji ki*" (Hokkien: 十二支, twelve sticks). He was a middle-aged, Teochew man who was *botak* (Malay: bald). We called him Uncle Botak Head.

The game is quite simple: if you wished to place a bet, you simply wrote two digits on a tiny piece of paper. All bets must come in one day before, and the results would be announced at noon the following day. The sums involved were not large and the chances of winning were definitely higher than 4D, which requires four digits. At the same time, the winnings were not huge either. Like many other housewives at that time, my mother often picked the numbers of her choice and scribbled them on a small piece of paper. She gave it to me, together with some coins, to pass to Uncle Botak Head.

Like now, housewives would pick their numbers based on some special event that occurred or on interpretations of their dreams. For example, if there was a wedding, the age of the bride and bridegroom could be considered good numbers to bet on. As for dreams, my mother would consider betting, for example, on the number four and two if she dreamed of two persons sitting at a table. Since a table has four legs and there were two persons — the logic goes — the number to buy was "42". There were of course various other interpretations for which I am no expert.

Uncle Botak Head was not the only guy taking such illegal bets. However, as the years passed, the government took a more serious stance against such illegal gambling activities and the *chap ji ki* syndicates eventually faded into oblivion.

Hawkers

Next to the market was a narrow passageway where hawkers sold cooked food. This is somewhat similar to our present-day food centres, except that it was neither as organized nor as clean. Food such as fishball noodle soup and *wonton mee* (Cantonese: 云吞面, dumpling noodles) were sold there. There was also an Indian stall or "mama stall" as it was called then, selling *teh tarik* (Malay: "pulled" milk tea) and *kopi susu* (Malay: coffee with milk), my elder brother's favourite.

I loved going there not for fried *mee* or fried *kway teow*, but for a type of banana cake. The cake usually took the shape of a banana, a doll or a cat! It was baked using charcoal instead of gas or electric ovens and always tasted delicious. Sadly, it has been years since I have come across this type of cake. Another of my favourite foods then was *char siew* (Cantonese: 叉烧, barbecued pork). My grandmother used to pamper me with 20 cents worth of this as I was her favourite grandchild.

One other food item we children loved very much was colourful ice balls. Ice was first compressed into a ball with bare hands and different syrups then added to create a vibrantly coloured ball. There was red bean at the centre of the ball, and milk was sometimes added to its surface. Because bare hands were used to shape the ice (there were no rubber gloves at that time), the health authorities put a stop to the sale of the ice balls. Ice kacang, served in a bowl instead, became more popular. While this is surely a more civilised way to enjoy the dessert, the fun of eating from a ball of ice is lost. What a pity indeed!

There was a stall that sold our favourite Hainanese "*tze char*" *kway teow*. It was located near the wet market across the canal from our flat at the night market, what we would consider a food centre today. Each plate of *kway teow* from that store cost between 50 cents to a dollar. Although it was slightly more expensive than the other type of fried *kway teow*, there were more ingredients in "*tze char*" *kway teow*.

We called the other type of *kway teow* "black and white" *kway teow*. This was the stall nearer our flat, and was located just at the corner of our opposite block. This hawker operated his stall from a timber cart. This type of hawker was a common sight in all parts of Singapore in the 1960s. The stall stayed open from about 7 o'clock in the evening till late at night. Each plate of fried *kway teow* came with fresh cockles and *lap cheong* (Cantonese: 腊肠, Chinese sausage) and cost only 20 cents without egg and 30 cents with egg. There were no styrofoam boxes or waxed paper for takeaways then. Instead, the food was wrapped with *opeh* leaves, and was tied with thin cane, not raffia, string.

Because my family was not well-to-do, we patronized the two food stalls only when Mother won *chap ji ki* or when Father had some extra cash from working overtime. Even then, we could only afford to buy two or three packets of food at a time. With chopsticks in hand and old newspapers laid out neatly on the floor as a makeshift dining table, everyone at home got to enjoy a few mouthfuls of the *kway teow* as the occasional supper, dinner having been taken in the early evening. Meagre as it was then, such informal food gatherings brought warmth and cheer to all family members.

Like the stall selling fried *kway teow*, all the stalls made use of kerosene lamps to light up their businesses at night. There was a water supply but a good number of stalls used pails to contain water for cooking and cleaning. Foldable tables, chairs and stools were all made of timber; plastic chairs and tables were not invented yet, neither were there plastic forks, spoons or disposable chopsticks. Chopsticks we used were made of wood while the containers we brought to the hawker to hold our fishball noodle soup were made of metal. Unlike now when plasticware is the norm, food in those days was always served in porcelain bowls, plates and cups, even at hawker stalls. There were no fast food chains like McDonald's or KFC back then. People mainly consumed local hawker food. During those early days, hawker food could be unhealthy and unhygienic, but surely it was more affordable and definitely much more delicious than what we have now.

Itinerant hawkers were also a common sight at the Blue Windows. I remember vividly an elderly Malay Satay Man, who wore a traditional *sarong* and a *songkok*, who came to our estate, mostly during the weekends, to sell his delicious satay. During those early years, satay was mostly sold by the Malays just as roti prata was sold by the Indians. The Malay Satay Man would usually call at about dinner time, carrying a wooden pole with two small timber cabinets hanging at each end of the pole. He used to station himself at the badminton court and start a makeshift barbecue fire. We could choose from chicken, lamb, and beef satay. His satay was grilled over red-hot charcoal in a homemade stove and was accompanied by a delicious but spicy peanut gravy that contained mashed pineapple. Another interesting aspect about satay stalls at that time is that most hawkers would charge their customers by counting the number of satay sticks there were after the meal. Naturally, there were cases of dishonest customers who secretly hid or threw away the sticks before the Satay Man counted them. Eventually, this practice was discontinued when the Satay Men wisened up!

The Satay Man was a true itinerant hawker who moved around the neighbourhood to sell his food. An old colleague of my father's once celebrated his birthday in his terrace house near our flat and invited the Satay Man to serve his guests. We were so surprised to see him there when we went to the house. The only food we had that evening was satay. Despite the lack of variety, we thoroughly enjoyed the meal, which included *ketupats* (Malay: rice cakes) in satay gravy and Red Spot orange drinks in glass bottles.

I also recall how we children would wait eagerly almost every afternoon for a middle-aged Indian man to pass by our flat. He had a very special way of carrying the basket of bread that he sold: he placed them on his white turbaned head. It was indeed fascinating that he could move his head from side to side as he talked to his customers, even with that basket-load of bread on his head. Whenever we wanted to buy bread, we would call out to him and use rope to lower a basket from our first floor flat. The friendly bread seller would place the bread inside the basket, after which we would retrieve the basket and take out the bread. We would put coins in its place and lower the basket down again to the bread seller. This common practice is interesting in retrospect and reflected the simplicity of life at that time; the bread seller trusted that we would pay him in good faith. Like all our neighbours, we did so every time. However, it is clearly no longer feasible to continue this practice today, not with the more suspicious nature of people living in our urbanized society today. Besides, lowering a basket in this manner from a twenty-storey HDB flat is simply unthinkable now!

That Indian man was not the only bread seller at that time. There was also a middle-aged Chinese uncle who sold his homemade bread from a wooden cabinet mounted at the back of his bicycle. Inside that cabinet was white bread and an assortment of spreads such as kaya, peanut butter, and of course butter and margarine.

When my uncle visited us, he liked to order *yong tau foo* and Chinese *rojak* from a particular hawker who came by our estate during dinner time. His deep fried *yong tau foo* was very tasty and I have not yet found another stall that can match his food in terms of texture, taste, and of course price. We also had the *Kok Kok Tng* Man, who sold a type of Chinese sweet. He would use short metal sticks to make sounds while carrying his stuff at the back seat of his bicycle. Another prominent mobile hawker was the Indian *Kacang Puteh* Man who sold all sorts of baked nuts and beans, which were placed in cones made of old newspaper. We could get a paper cone of nuts and beans for just five cents! During those days, buying cones of *kacang puteh* when we went to the cinemas was a must. Without it in hand, something always seemed to be missing from the fun of seeing a movie.

But of all these pushcarts and unlicensed hawkers, two of them left a lasting impression in my mind for their uniqueness and creativity. One of them was an old man who sold *muah chee* (Hokkien: 麻糍 glutinious rice), a kind of sticky Chinese snack made of flour and white sugar. He really loved children and was always singing and dancing while selling his *muah chee*, voluntarily turning himself into a sort of clown just to entertain his customers, who were mostly young children and old folks. I still remember the English rhymes he used to sing. They sound something like this:

One, two, tighten my shoe,
Three, four, lock the door,
Five, six, pick a stick,
Seven, eight, knock your head,
Nine, ten, pitch a tent!

He would sing and dance at the same time and the children would laughingly gather around him. A welcomed sight indeed at the Blue Windows!

The other hawker who formed a lasting impression was the young boy who took orders of Hokkien prawn *mee*. He went around the estate alerting potential customers with the "tit tot" sound he created by hitting two short bamboo sticks together. He would then rush back to the stall after an order was placed and come back later with the bowls of noodles on a tray. It was the equivalent of a home delivery service. Once, my brother ordered the *mee*, then a mere 20 cents a bowl, for all of us in celebration after winning five dollars in a riddle contest organized by Rediffusion Singapore. And so the boy brought all of us bowls of noodles on a Saturday afternoon. He would come back a while later to collect the empty bowls. Such was the practice then, when trust and honesty were the order of the day.

The old farmer

During the early days of the 1960s, sanitary conditions, even in government-built housing such as ours, were in no way comparable to what we have today. It was quite common then for the nearby farmers to collect leftovers from households to use as feed for their livestock. To facilitate this, Mother would put all the unwanted leftovers from lunch and dinner in a metal container for an old farmer to collect the next day. The next morning at around ten o'clock, an elderly farmer from Boh Beh Kang kampung would come to our house to collect the leftovers. Such unhygienic practices were prevalent at that time at the Blue Windows and in other parts of Singapore as well.

That elderly old farmer owned chicken and pig farms and would use these leftovers to feed his livestock. We addressed him as "old uncle". He was a kind man and walked with a slight limp. He used to wear shorts and singlets but his untidy attire and body odour meant that we children were terrified of going near him. As a form of appreciation, every family who contributed their leftovers would receive a live chicken from him nearing Chinese New Year. Over the years, this reciprocal kindness meant that the old man became a friend to all the neighbours at the Blue Windows. Once, I refused to let him in when he brought a chicken to my house and I was alone. When Mother came back from the market, the old man was waiting outside our house and actually told Mother that I was smart enough not to let a stranger into the house!

Although the chicken inevitably ended up slaughtered for the reunion dinner, we really looked forward to receiving our temporary pet of a few days. It was fun and served as a curiosity for us children. It also proved to be a challenging time for my parents since no one in the family actually dared to kill the bird. In the end, my uncle took up the challenge and knifed the bird at its neck but without much success. The poor bird lived on for quite a while before it passed out due to excessive bleeding. After that incident, and also because it felt cruel eating a chicken that had lived with us for a few days, my parents decided to bring the chickens to the hawker at the wet market in exchange for readily-slaughter bird. Of course, we had to forgo a big bird in return for a smaller one.

The neighbourhood shops

Across the "white bridge", so named because it was always painted white, was a row of single-storey shophouses. Near our house, at the corner of the row was a Hainanese coffee shop. Father used to have coffee there on many evenings after dinner. Sometimes, he would bring me along and have me sit beside him. To save money, he would order just one cup of coffee with milk and share it with me by pouring some on the cup saucer for me to drink. Up till now, I still have vivid memories of what the shop looked liked, the marble table top, the overhead ceiling fans and the spittoon located below each table. Even the chairs were made of solid teak, a luxury not afforded nowadays in our present day coffee shops. The boss of the coffee shop was an old Hainanese man and sold tasty toast with kaya and butter.

At other times, Father would ask me to buy coffee from there. During those days, we had to bring our own

A provision shop along Strathmore Avenue, Block 46, in the early 1980s. It has since been torn down.

containers, such as a pot made of iron or our own cups, to take coffee away. Alternatively, the coffee shop's owner would pour the coffee into used metal milk tins, with its cover tied to a fibre string. There was no such thing as plastic bags or nylon string then.

This row of single-storey shophouses included a laundry shop, which was owned by a Hakka family and occupied the corner unit. There was also a photo studio that we frequented very often, especially during the Chinese New Year period, to take our family pictures. Ng Kee Grocery Shop, our only shopping destination at the Blue Windows, was also located there. Next to Ng Kee was a unit that was shared between a barber and women's hair salon. The barber shop occupied half the unit while the other half was occupied by a lady's hair salon. During those days, there were no unisex hair salons like what we have now.

The main shopping and commercial area

Down the road from Margaret Drive was our first air-conditioned shopping centre, Queenstown Shopping Complex. It was a three-storey standalone building. My parents liked to take evening walks there after dinner and go shopping there during the weekends.

On the ground floor were small, individual shops, which included a wrist watch shop and Mont' De Cake Shop, which specialized in "western-style" cakes. This cake shop holds special memories for my siblings and me because it gave us our first taste of "western-style" cake, with cream and various toppings. Prior to that, the only type of "cake" we knew of was the *kueh nerng kor* (Teochew: 鸡蛋糕, steamed egg cakes) that Mother and Grandmother baked. According to Father, the shop was owned by his company, Sime Darby. Unfortunately, it was replaced by another operation a few years later.

On the second storey of the complex was Tah Chung Emporium, one of Singapore's earliest departmental stores. With its opening, business at the local provision shops took a beating as many people started to make purchases from the Emporium instead. Tah Chung mainly sold made-in-China products and its interior was filled with goods ranging from clothing, household utensils and electrical goods. It was the first time we children had seen so many products housed under one roof. On the third storey was a nightclub and Golden Crown Restaurant, a famous Chinese dining establishment.

There were also two cinemas next to the emporium: Golden City Cinema and Venus Cinema. Both screened mainly Chinese and Cantonese films from Taiwan and Hong Kong respectively. What was interesting was that the cinemas also screened graduation ceremonies of

neighbouring schools! The two cineplexes made Queenstown seem even more hip and exciting. Itinerant hawkers
would gather near the fountain in front of the cinemas to
catch the film-going crown.

Tah Chung and the smaller shops did quite well up
to the middle of the 1970s, when NTUC opened its own
chain of supermarkets in Singapore. By then, private
emporiums started to face increasingly stiff competition and after a while, the emporium closed down. An
empty plot of land remains where Queenstown Shopping
Complex once stood. A number of the other smaller oper-
ations either relocated or followed suit. Competition from
newer cineplexes likewise forced the two cinemas to close
in 1984. Their premises was eventually used by church
organisations, but were later abandoned.

One building in that once "happening" area that
remains today is the Queenstown Public Library. It has
been standing for 43 years and is the first public library
built in the heartlands of Singapore. Luckily, its exterior
has remained mostly unchanged. Since it stayed open till
9 o'clock at night, like many of the other students from
the many schools along Margaret Drive in the 1970s, I
used to spend hours studying at the small but cosy library
after school. I used to go there with some of my classmates who also stayed at the Blue Windows and our visits
became especially frequent nearing the exams.

The barber

A vivid memory of my growing up years was having my
hair cut in a dimly-lit barber shop. The shop was run by a
Chinese middle-aged barber who also cut my father's hair.
Most, if not all, of the barbers in those days were Chinese
or Indian middle-aged men. Women went to hair salons

run by self-taught hairdressers to have their hair permed or cut. Some women even had their hair done up by female hairdressers who would come to their flats. Big hairdos were the norm in those times and my mother's hairstyle was no exception.

When it was time for me to have my hair cut, my mother would bring me to that barber shop while she went to the adjoining hair salon to have her hair permed. During such visits, the barber would sit me on a raised timber plank that was placed across the handles of the barber chair. Then he would use an old pair of scissors and rusty mechanical hair clippers to trim off what little hair I had. When I was done with my haircut, I would go next door to look for my mother. Typically, the aunties there would be gossiping about various families and everything under the sun. I loathed it when the hairdresser serving mother liked to pass unflattering comments about my nearly *botak* head, just to evoke laughter among those in the salon. Most of the time, I could not even understand what they were saying since they spoke in Cantonese. Nonetheless, the sweet titbits that the lady boss always offered me made up for the mild humiliation. When I started attending secondary school, I decided to go to the Indian barber just to escape being the unwitting subject of the gossiping aunties.

The "dentist"

When we had toothaches, Mother would bring us to an unregistered dentist who practised in his house along Dawson Lane as it was much cheaper. The "dentist" was a middle-aged family man who worked as an assistant in a government dental clinic but moonlighted as a dentist in his free time, mostly during the evening and on weekends. We were accompanied by Mother each time we visited him, which was often on a Sunday morning. His three-room flat was on the ground floor of a four-storey apartment block, quite near to the wet market, and I can still remember the tiny garden with a variety of plants outside his house. Dental procedures were carried out in his kitchen among his wife's pots and pans. There was neither a proper dental chair nor a white coat, things that we now expect dentists to use. Instead, he wore a short-sleeved shirt and long pants and walked around the flat barefooted. This was in those early years when legislation on medical and dental practices was not as strict as it is today.

Besides filling in our decayed teeth, the "dentist" also performed extraction. Despite the fact that he was an unregistered practitioner, his skill was excellent. But sad to say, instead of proper dental treatment, the decision to just extract the tooth was often taken when I had a toothache. This resulted in a lot of my teeth being gone in no time. I had to put on plastic dentures during my teenage years. My siblings and parents suffered the same fate as me.

Ironically, when I was in my Secondary Three, I quite liked the idea of going to the dentist's house because I was infatuated with one of his four daughters, a studious Secondary Two girl. She was petite but aloof, and I found her pretty and charming, especially with her long hair and her gracious manner. We hardly talked to one another. Unfortunately, I did not garner the courage to approach her and it remained a one-sided affair, an incident of puppy love. I guess her dentist father would have known what to do with my teeth if he found out about my secret admiration for his daughter!

CHAPTER 2

IN THE HOUSE

Home décor

In the 1960s and early 1970s, almost all the government-built flats at the Blue Windows comprised of rental units. Since most people rented their flats or houses, they had no long-term commitment to the place and very few people spent money on decorating or renovating their flats. Most of the time, tenants just made do with a basic touch-up. The only house decoration we had back in Queenstown were some homemade decorative shrimps, made with plastic string wrapped around marbles. These were hung on our white wall. Even the curtains at home were home-made and cannot compare to the lace curtains that we are accustomed to using today. Even with such rudimentary enhancements, people were happy and contented with their lot. People then were less particular about the interior décor of their homes, but most of our neighbours kept their house clean and tidy.

A simple and common example of decorative efforts was putting a layer of colourful mats over the bare concrete floor. Those rubber mats were a very common feature in most flats and were not bought from renovation contractors but from provision shops. Father bought ours from Ng Kee Provision Shop. The mats came in various colours and patterns and could only last for a few years. The family usually had to change them a few weeks before the Chinese New Year. If the floor was smooth, some households put a coat of enamel paint on their floor instead of laying the mats. There were not many specialist renovation or interior decoration businesses during those days and there was no ready market for such businesses. It was only in the late 1970s as a result of the public housing programmes in Toa Payoh and some other estates that renovation contractors and interior decoration businesses mushroomed in Singapore.

Salt refrigerators, charcoal stoves and a stone rice grinder

Our foods such as leftover dinner, fresh vegetables and even raw meat were stored in the *kiam sng tu* (Teochew: 咸冰橱, "salt refrigerator") that was placed in the kitchen. Even though the Chinese term literally meant "salt refrigerator", it was not a basic version of the modern electronic refrigerator but simply a wooden cabinet designated for keeping food. Obviously, food could not be kept there for long. This cupboard's four legs stood on four inverted porcelain bowls filled with salted water. This helped to prevent insects such as ants and cockroaches from climbing up the cupboard. To ensure that there was ventilation, the cupboard's panel was made of wire mesh. As the cupboard was made of timber, Mother put rubber mats on the shelves to prevent the surfaces from getting wet. It was only in the mid-1970s that we had our first electric refrigerator.

For cooking, we used charcoal for fuel instead of gas, which only became available in the middle of the 1970s. The use of open-air charcoal stoves required skill. Not only was it tedious to ignite the fire, it was hard to control

A stone rice grinder that is similar to the one Gao Chek owned, I came across this in Chen Ci Hong's Mansion, Shantou, China when I was there on a tour in 2009. The tourist attraction continues to draw Overseas Chinese of Teochew descent who are curious about their past.

the amount of heat necessary for whatever food was being cooked. Nowadays, we only use charcoal at barbeques but all these came naturally to the housewives of those days. It also seems to me that food cooked over a charcoal fire tastes better!

The heavily, circular, stone rice grinder (Chinese: 石磨, *shi mo*) was a traditional implement that was commonly used during those days to produce rice flour for making traditional rice cakes or Teochew *kway*. Being poor, we did not own one. However, Gao Chek, a Teochew *poong tor* seller (Teochew: 潮州饭粿, rice dumpling), owned one of the best stone grinders in our estate. My mother was pleased that he was always kind enough to let her use the grinder for short periods. As such, my grandmother and my mother would go to a neighbour's house during festive seasons such as Chinese New Year to use their stone grinder to manually grind polished rice into a starchy or powdery form.

When Mother or Grandma was in their house, we children would chip in to help turn the handle of the *shimo*. Of course, we did not do it for long as it was heavy and it was a rather tedious task. While grinding the white rice, the womenfolk would inevitably engage in leisurely small talk about domestic issues and other trivial matters. In retrospect, those were the little moments that fostered the good relations among neighbours.

The bathroom

Our bathroom was very basic, with concrete flooring and walls. In fact, we did not even know how ceramic tiles looked like in those early years. While we did have piped water, we did not have modern-day luxuries like a shower head or bathroom accessories. Most families simply used a big earthen pot to collect water for bathing and washing. It was refreshing to bathe with water that had been left overnight in such pots. In fact, I still keep one of these porcelain earthen pots in my bathroom as a standby supply of water at home. Despite having to share a single toilet and bathroom with more than ten persons, we were comparatively fortunate. I heard that families living in *attap* huts in the nearby Bukit Ho Swee still had to use the dug well for water and made use of a hole in the ground as a toilet.

When it came to personal hygiene, the same square bar of soap was used for washing our body, our hair and even our clothes. Of course, before the washing machine arrived in the 70s, all laundry had to be done by hand. Wooden washing boards with grooves were also available, making the chore easier for housewives.

Our sleeping arrangements

My sisters and parents shared one bedroom while Grandma and Small Aunt shared the other. The rooms were small especially when partitioned with makeshift curtains. My two older brothers and I slept in the living room at night. To maximize the use of the space, Father bought three foldable canvas beds. It became a ritual to take the beds out every night and lay them side by side in the hall and pack up again in the morning and return them to the balcony where they were stored. It may sound troublesome, but we got used to this little ritual and came to enjoy it.

Bedding items we used also had their own unique flavour. For example, my grandmother used a hard, timber lacquered pillow. Apparently, it encouraged blood circulation and had been in use for a long time in China. To this day, I remain puzzled by how she managed to fall asleep. We children used normal cotton pillows and blankets. These were all homemade. Bits of leftover cloth were stitched together to form a quilt. The result was a colourful and soft blanket that provided enough warmth for a good night's sleep. In those days, this was done to save cost. Similar blankets are still available nowadays; perhaps it is the beautiful mosaic of colours and styles that makes it attractive to consumers today.

This was how we lived during those childhood days; days when life was so simple that even our clothes and our underwear were made at home by our mother. Also, a pair of leather shoes would last for a long time in those days. Indeed, very few people living at the Blue Windows in those days could afford luxury goods and if they could, they had few choices since there were not that many major shopping centres in Singapore, least of all in the Queenstown area.

Me in the mid-1960s. The cardboard box on the shelf behind me contained our first home telephone.

Our first home telephone

Modern — or rather what we then considered "modern" — gadgets began to surface in the late 60s and early 70s. My family got our first home telephone in 1969 when I was in Secondary Three. Everyone at home was excited and wanted to learn how to use it. It was not the first time we had seen a telephone since most of us knew about the rotary telephone at the provision shop; Father must have used one in his office as well. Yet, when the Telephone Man came to our house to install the all-black, round-dial gauge telephone, we were very proud of it. But like country bumpkins we were too frightened to use it since we found it strange to talk to a box and not a human. One of my younger sisters once ran to hide in the room when the telephone rang, generating much laughter from the rest of the family. Of course, all of us became used to the telephone in due course and it slowly become indispensible at home. In the mid 1970s, our old round-dial gauge telephone was replaced with a light-grey, push button telephone.

Rediffusion radio and the gramophone

The MP3 or iPhone were unheard of then and we only had Rediffusion Singapore and the transistor radio, a limited choice indeed. On certain evenings, my brothers and I would listen to the Rediffusion broadcast of ghost stories and scare ourselves to sleep. Small Aunt used to listen to a Teochew story-telling programme on Rediffusion, hosted by Mr. Ng Chia Ken, when she was preparing dinner for us in the evenings. The stories were usually about olden-day warriors and were related to Chinese history. Since it was in dialect, I did not understand much of what he said. Even then, the cable radio service was an intrinsic part of our lives; perhaps because the television was non-existent and the radio hard to come by in those early days in Singapore.

One day, my uncle brought home a gramophone set out of the blue. We were all fascinated by the beautiful sound that came out of the box with a turnable record. I laughingly recall how ignorant I was as a boy when I asked my uncle if there was anyone hiding in the box singing the songs. To my surprise, my uncle answered in the affirmative and encouraged me to find the singer by propping me up to look more closely into the lighted box. I did as instructed, but to my frustration, could find no one!

Television sets and RTS

Another evening, my father returned home after work at Shenton Way to announce the advent of the modern television. He enthusiastically described how one could

Small Aunt adjusting the bulky radio that my uncle bought for us.

see people performing within a small lighted screen. The device came with sound too! After only a few months, Father managed to buy a 19-inch black-and-white television. It was a Hitachi that had a slightly convex, light green screen when it was turned off. When television first started, the only programmes that were available were produced by the government-run Radio and Television Singapore or RTS. RTS programmes were very well received since television was a novelty at that time.

Being one of the very first families to own a television, neighbours from near and far flocked to our tiny flat to watch television programmes. A few old ladies and men also made our flat their favourite meeting place to watch shows on the television, particularly black-and-white Teochew operas, as well as other Hong Kong-produced soup operas. Another well received show was the Mandarin variety show "*Si Po Zi Yat*" (Cantonese: 声宝之夜, "Sharp Night") hosted by the compere Zheng Wei. As

The 14-inch, black-and-white television from our days at the Blue Windows. I keep this in my office.

for comedies, we had the famous dialect-speaking comedians, Wang Sa and Ye Fong. Wang Sa was a thin guy who spoke Teochew while Ye Fong was a fat one who spoke Cantonese and some broken English. Their shows were very funny and were naturally popular with the audience of the 1970s.

Of course, children were fond of watching TV shows that featured dogs, such as *Lassie* and *Rin Tin Tin*, action films such as *Robin Hood*, and entertainment shows such as the local English and Chinese Talentime. For cartoons, we had Porky Pig, Mickey Mouse and towards the mid-70s, Tom and Jerry. We also liked English adult programmes, especially spy films such as the James Bond franchise, the exciting police drama television series *Hawaii Five-O*, and the satirical secret agent series *Get Smart*. Initially, all TV programmes were in black-and-white, a few came with Chinese subtitles, and none were in stereo sound.

Mother in a nyonya kebaya with my three younger sisters. The black-and-white television and the small white refrigerator were our prized possessions.

During those early years, all television programmes ended at 9 o'clock in the evening. Two of Lau Gou's sons used to come over to our flat to watch the black-and-white television and were very often reluctant to go home even after the end of the transmission. They thought my father was lying to them about the programme timings to get them to go home! Unlike the hi-tech and innovative presentation today, news segments were uncreative and uninteresting and were simply presented with a news reader reading out the news, followed by short news streams. People were fascinated by TV sets but it must have been the beginning of a shift in the way of life, which diluted the kampung spirit of those early years. Eventually, more people would prefer to stay home to watch television rather than go out and visit neighbours. Not surprisingly,

The Konica camera that Father bought in the 1960s. It could only produce black and white photographs.

movie attendance suffered because of the convenience of home entertainment and a number of cinemas ended up closing down.

Early cameras and typewriters

During festive seasons such as Chinese New Year, Father would use a very old-fashioned, made-in-Japan Konica camera. Still, it was considered quite advanced in comparison to the other models available such as the Seagull Camera (海鸥碑照相机) from China. Of course, in those early years, photographs were in black and white. We had to bring the roll of film to a photo studio to be developed into physical, printed photographs.

Of all the things we used in those days, the gadget that most fascinated me must have been the manual typewriter. These machines were bulky. Being one of the very few

45

English-educated guys around during that time, my father owned one. Father used to type both official and personal letters on his device. Ink ribbons were about half an inch wide and usually came in black or black and red. Occasionally, we even had green ribbon. Sometimes the ribbon got jammed up and we had to spend a lot of time trying to untangle the mess. Of course, the end result of the type-written printout is in no way comparable to the quality of inkjet or laser printers, but we made do with what we had. To make multiple copies, one would place carbon paper below the original sheet. Trying to make corrections to multiple copies, as you can imagine, was always a tedious task. There was also no such thing as the cut-and-paste function. If there was a mistake, we had to use an ink eraser to make amendments. It was only in the late 70s that correction paper and subsequently correction fluid were invented.

My father insisted that I learn how to use the type-writer properly. He taught me how to use the correct finger for each respective alphabet. It was through such early training that I was able to type at a relatively fast rate even without looking at the keytop. It is also this skill that enabled me to use the personal computer later on in my life. While I am grateful to my father for imparting this skill to me, I am sure he too was very proud of having a son who was able to help him out in both his work and his brother's business. The electric and electronic typewriters came after the mechanical ones. Some of these typewriters are still available today but are clearly being overlooked in favour of the all-powerful personal computers. At the end of the day, however, it is the old mechanical typewriter I grew up with that I still think of fondly.

An old mechanical typewriter. My father-in-law gave it to my wife in the early 1970s.

Wrist watches, school bags and fountain pens

There were basically two types of school bags in the 1960s. Primary school students used what Teochew people called "*kek*" bags. This was probably a direct translation from the English word "cardboard" since the bag was actually made of cardboard with a layer of cloth covering it and vinyl in the corners. Besides the *kek* bags, there was also the more traditional type of bag made of canvas cloth; these were usually used by secondary school students. These sling bags came in green or beige. Both my two older brothers carried them while I carried my *kek* bag. Inside the school bags, we would have our wooden pencil box, rulers, "rubbers", and sometimes crayons and water colours. We had simple needs and considered it a joy to get new stationery, especially during the beginning of the school term.

Wrist watches were treasured possessions and were sought-after as gifts in the 1970s. I fondly remember my

The "kek" bag that younger school children used.

first watch, a Timex, a gift from my father for doing well during my Secondary Two examinations. That watch was unlike electronic watches. The mechanical gears within the bulky watch meant you could hear it ticking if you placed it close to your ears. Despite this, I was so pleased upon getting my first wrist watch that I wore it day and night for many months.

Most people wrote with fountain pens, the most common brands being Parker and Sheaffer. Then ballpoint pens arrived in the mid-1970s. The brand BIC should be familiar to those who were in their teens then. Somehow, my father insisted that we stick to using the fountain pen as he believed that the use of ballpoint pens would affect our handwriting adversely. Nevertheless, as time went on, everyone started to use the ballpoint pen and the fountain pen became less popular with schoolchildren.

CHAPTER 3

FAMILY, FRIENDS AND NEIGHBOURS

Our clothes

In our circle of relatives, friends and neighbours, people went about their daily lives wearing whatever they could lay their hands on. For men, it usually meant long cotton pants and white long-sleeved shirts rolled up to the elbows. My father dressed in this manner when he went to work. Women wore *samfoo* (Cantonese: 衫裤): two-piece outfits consisting of homemade slacks and a short-sleeved blouse that looked very much like pyjamas. The cloth from which the *samfoo* was cut came in various floral patterns and seemed to be very comfortable. Like most other married women at the Blue Windows, this was the way my mother dressed at home or when she went to the wet market.

For the older generation, such as the *ah peh* (Teochew: 阿伯, old uncles) or the *ah mm* (Teochew 阿妈: old aunties) the dress style was quite different. An *ah peh* would usually put on a loose pair of white or black cotton trousers that was tightened with a belt around his waist and an open neck Chinese singlet. An *ah mm* like my grandmother would usually be dressed in a pair of black slacks and a light blue blouse. Her hair would also be tied into a bun at the back of her head. These were the ways old people in China dressed and this dress sense remained in our society then.

Boys would put on shorts and a singlet or an old short-sleeved shirt while girls would put on homemade dresses. Mother had learnt dressmaking from her father who was a tailor, and catered to my sisters' clothing needs. In fact, during those early years, it was common practice for older siblings to pass their clothing on to their younger siblings year after year. Unfortunately, it now seems like there is wanton wastage in the way youngsters discard their clothing once fashion trends are over. As I was growing up, my generation was taught to be thrifty and treasure what little belongings — such as the few pairs of trousers or shirts — we possessed. Besides, it must be noted that most of the people would only buy new clothes nearing Chinese New Year. Clothes vendors had a hard time running their businesses for the rest of the year since most people had limited spending power. For most people, even their underwear and pyjamas were home-made. Yet, these simple items were as comfortable as the expensive, branded undergarments and clothes that are available today.

As the economy improved, fashion for women and men began to surface in the middle of the 1970s. Despite the general conservativism, miniskirts that were trendy in western countries began to attract the interest of local women and, if I may add, men! It was common for school girls to be sent home because of the inappropriate length of their school skirts. If miniskirts appealed to the ladies, bell-bottomed pants appealed to the young men. In fact, the wider the bell bottom, the "groovier" it was. On top of that, the influence of hippie culture in the West meant that sporting long hair among men became trendy. The prevalence of these "bad" trends gave the school head-masters a headache. During my secondary school days, one of the many duties of the prefects (I happened to be one myself) was to catch fellow students with long hair. The benchmark for this was hair that covered both the student's ears. Once a student, usually a guy was caught, the school master would give him a hasty and rough haircut. Quite often, this was carried out in front of the other students during assembly time. During those early years, parents were respectful of the school principals and teachers; complaints for taking disciplinary action were almost unheard of.

Besides bell-bottomed long trousers, our shirts at that time came with high collars. It was also very common in the 1970s for people to have their shirts or trousers tailor-made. At that time, there were no big shopping centres or mass-produced clothes and tailors were running a very good business. I, for one, was influenced by one of my primary school classmates, Wei Kiong, who came from a relatively well-to-do family. His father was a sailor and earned quite a high salary. Though Wei Kiong was young, he was very particular about his attire. One day, he asked me to follow him to the famous CYC tailor where he was going to have a shirt and a pair of trousers made. With my father's permission, I also had a shirt with a high collar made.

With some exceptions, most people in those days did not place much emphasis on their dressing. Most regular people were struggling to make a living and could not afford to indulge in fashion. However, Western influence dominated professional work attire and businessmen still put on coats and ties despite the hot and humid weather. High society ladies also attended formal functions and parties in gowns and heavy make-up. The influence of the motherland — China for the Chinese and India for the Indian immigrants — was more obvious then. What we consider "ethnic clothing" now was typical then, Sikh turbans were commonplace and Chinese women wore *cheongsam* (Cantonese: 长衫) or *qipao* (Chinese: 旗袍) on a regular basis. Such diversity in everyday dressing reflected our multi-racial society.

Our lingo

My mother was a born linguist. Before she married my father, Mother stayed in the Selegie Road area where many of her neighbours were Cantonese and Peranakan. In addition to Teochew, she spoke fluent Cantonese and Pasar Melayu, an informal Malay dialect commonly heard at the wet markets. However, she did not understand a word of English. Father was educated in Mandarin and English. He also spoke some Japanese because he was a teenager during the Occupation and had learnt some Japanese at school. Despite learning Mandarin in school, Father could not speak it fluently. He could, however, read and write it well enough to understand literary Chinese and classical Chinese works such as poems by poets such Li Bai (李白). His Cantonese accent was also slightly awkward and we would all laugh whenever he spoke it.

Most people in our community spoke various dialects to one another. It is hard to appreciate how differently people communicated with one another then. Although Singapore had achieved independence from Malaysia by 1965, national identity was very much still in its infancy and there was no notion of a common language. In small estates like the Blue Windows, most people normally belonged to one or two prominent dialect groups. Most of the neighbours were either Teochew or Hokkien, with a smattering of Cantonese and Hakka families.

But even in those early years, our dialects were mixed with words and phrases from Malay and sometimes English. For example, when my mother said that she was going to the market, she would say she was going to the *pasar*. Or when my father stayed at home for a day, he would say he had taken "*cuti*" (Malay: holiday), in other words, he was on leave. Another example of the profusion of Malay words into our dialect is how "*mata*" (Malay: literally "eye") referred to the policeman. When we were naughty as children, Grandma would say that the *mata* would come to catch us. With such refrains, the children of yesteryear were trained to be afraid of policemen from young.

Other Malay phrases and the ways we used them are as follow:

Teruk meant tough
E.g., His work load was very *teruk* so he had to work really had.

Susah was used to express disappointment
E.g., She messed up my work, *susah* lah! I have to do it all over again.

Lain macam literally meant "of a special kind" and was used to show disapproval for someone
E.g., He was invited to our party. But he refused to come, he is such a *lain macam* person!

Panjang referred to a tall person
E.g., *Panjang* Ah Kow is a friend of mine.

Katik referred to a short person
E.g., He is so *katik* that he was not selected for his school basketball team.

Our colloquialisms were also influenced by English words. For example, when a patient in the hospital asked the "missy" or "bisi" for a cup of warm water, he was asking for the nurse. The word "missy/bisi" very likely derived from the polite English word, "Miss". Chinese people could not pronounce or use the word properly and so ended up with the pronunciation "missy" or "bisi" to refer specifically to the nurse, especially since nurses in those days were predominantly female. It seems like the term "missy/bisi" has survived the test of time and older persons still use this term to refer to nurses. While on the road, when the *laybar* — a near pronunciation of *drebar* (Malay: driver) — said that he wanted to "gostan", he meant was that he wanted to reverse the car. "Gostan" could be a derivation of the English phrase, "to go astern", which refers to a backwards movement. Such unique conversational ways would only be understood by the locals. An Englishman, a Malay person or even a Chinese person from the mainland China would have had a hard time understanding such mixed language/dialect conversation.

The term "Singlish" was unheard of at that time. But there was no doubt that the way languages were spoken then eventually evolved into what we now call Singlish. It is intriguing how people from different dialect groups or races could understand these expressions easily. These localized ways of speaking were passed down to the present generation. However, with the Speak Mandarin Campaign (1979) that discouraged the use of dialect, and the passing of the older generation of Singaporeans, some colourful dialect expressions will most probably die a natural death. That will be a great loss to our various cultural roots and collective Singaporean identity.

The cars of the 1970s

There were not many privately-owned cars on the roads in the 1970s. Most were European brands such as Austin, Ford and of course, Mercedes Benz and Japanese brands had only started to penetrate the local motor vehicle

My younger brother and me beside the Ford my eldest brother bought

market. Our upstairs neighbour bought a new Mazda Saloon, which was sleek and impressive. It was only in the early 1970s, soon after my elder brother left school to work as a salesman at Sime Darby, that my family could afford a second-hand car. Father bought a light blue Ford Prefect with a really solid body from his friend, a used car dealer. Unfortunately, its interior conditions, broken leather seats and shaky steering, were less attractive. It looked old in comparison to our neighbour's brand new car but we were quite happy to have a car of our own nonetheless.

Prior to getting our own Ford, we used to get rides in my uncle's black Morris Minor, which he used for work. The most interesting feature of that little Morris must have been the pop out signals by the side of the windows on both sides of the car. When Uncle wanted to signal that he was turning left, he would press a button on the dashboard, and the signal lever on the left side of the steering wheel would pop out. If he wanted to signal right, the one on right side would pop out. I cannot remember what he had to do to turn on the hazard lighting. During those years, cars did not have any built-in air conditioners; it was only in the later part of the 1970s that drivers could fix their cars up with a modular air conditioner.

A failed romance

My uncle lived with his workers at his electrical shop along Boat Quay. When I was in primary school, he started dating Small Aunt's close friend, whom we called Siok Keng *Go* (Teochew: 姑, aunty). Aunty Siok Keng was English-educated, just like my father. He held her in high regard and liked her cultured manner. I looked forward to her visiting with Uncle as she would speak to me in English. Other than Father, who was often busy, I could not practise my English with anyone at home. Despite the age gap, we were quite happy to practise English together. I thought she would make a good teacher — at least she was better than the ones who taught me in school. Our whole family, especially my grandmother and we children were very fond of her as she was always very gentle and friendly.

I was too young then to understand the world of love and romantic feelings, but years later, Mother told me that it was Aunty Siok Keng who fell in love with my uncle first and initiated getting close to him and our family. This was considered a very bold move for a young woman during the 1960s and 1970s. Perhaps there was a personality clash or an incompatibility of educational backgrounds but the two of them eventually broke off their relationship after a period of courtship. Though my uncle was handsome, he was also unpolished especially in comparison to the soft-spoken and well-mannered Aunty Siok Keng. Moreover, he was not a learned person and spoke very little English while Aunty Siok Keng was English-educated. My uncle did not seem to treasure her intelligence and charm. When Aunty Siok Keng bought a cake for my grandmother's birthday, he criticised her, saying it was a waste of money.

Uncle was not in the least perturbed after their relationship ended. Perhaps he had been emotionally troubled but did not show it openly? That was unlikely since he was the one who called it off. Father was disappointed with his younger brother for missing an opportunity to marry a good woman like Aunty Siok Keng. However, Uncle soon found himself a new girlfriend from a well-to-do Teochew family in Hougang. He married her and rented a room near our flat. As for Aunty Siok Keng, we were told that she married a Malaysian man and settled down in Sarawak. We heard that she passed away in the course of a miscarriage a few years later and were saddened by the news.

My "aunty" and godparents

My eldest aunt worked as an *amah* (Hokkien: 阿嬤, live-in domestic servant) for a Peranakan family. She stayed with her gardener-husband in the servants' quarter in a bungalow somewhere in the prestigious Tanglin area. Occasionally, my parents would hail a pirate taxi and bring us to visit her. I was also very fascinated by the big garden in their *jiak hong chu* (Teochew: 吃风屋, "eat wind house"), a term used to refer to luxurious bungalows.

We understood that my aunt's boss had a high position at a big factory that manufactured Ovaltine. Her employer was kind to us when we visited Eldest Aunt, leaving her to talk to us alone. Of course, my parents were also careful not to cause too much inconvenience to Eldest Aunt and her employer. Despite being invited to enter the main house, they kept such visits short and usually confined themselves to the workers' quarters where Aunty and her husband lived. I was not keen on following my parents there as her employer had a few fierce-looking dogs, whose barks were frightening and uninviting.

As children, we were very well-behaved and did not dare do anything that would disturb their employer. Eldest Aunt and her husband had four children and even then, we could feel the difference in culture between them and us. For one thing, Eldest Aunt and Uncle were Peranakan Chinese (Straits-born Chinese), so their children spoke mainly Baba Malay and some English, while we conversed in our dialect, Teochew. Obviously, there was a communication gap.

Despite the fact that my aunt was just a servant, her employer treated her and her family very well. Indeed, they were treated as family. My grandmother and father were very happy for her in that respect. In fact, this Aunt of ours was not my grandmother's biological daughter but had been adopted when she was young. Even then, my grandmother treated her no differently from how she treated her other children. Besides, the love Eldest Aunt demonstrated for my grandmother was equal to if not more than what most daughters give their mothers. Such was the exemplary model that we naturally looked up to as young children.

One of the interesting practices during those early years must have been adopting one's aunt as a godmother. According to traditional beliefs in the Chinese zodiac where certain zodiac animals are more compatible with others, my younger brother who was born in the Year of the Pig had to get a godmother who was born in the Year of the Dragon. Since my eldest aunt met the criteria, she was naturally appointed by Grandma as the godmother to my younger brother. Since I was born in the Year of the Horse, Grandma did not require me to have any godparents. Grandma did not explain her decision-making process. To me, it simply meant that I did not get an extra *angpow* during Chinese New Year or on my birthday. My brother, of course, got one from his beloved godmother on both occasions.

A tab at Ng Kee

Supermarkets were unheard of then. It was only during the later part of the 70s that Tah Chung Emporium was set up along Margaret Drive, a stone's throw from our house. Prior to that, my parents usually purchased our daily necessities from Ng Kee Provision Shop. This shop was along the row of single storey shophouses that included the Hainanese coffee shop, the hairdresser and the photo studio. The boss, Mr. Ng, was running a very good business selling daily necessities to the residents of the Blue Windows. While my parents were busy placing their orders for our daily necessities with Mr. Ng, we children liked to run around the wide concrete pavement in front of the shops. At night, fluorescent tubes lit up the shops and the pavement, resulting in a relaxing atmosphere for the residents to mingle in. It was common then for customers to draft a buying list and have all the items delivered to their house by an employee of the shop. We were no exception. Once a month, Mr. Ng's employee would cycle to our flat with the groceries that Mother ordered on his bicycle's back basket.

At times, Father was short of cash and had to buy on credit. Mr. Ng was initially kind enough to accede to Father's requests and Father made payment promptly at the end of each month. However, there was an incident that left Father deeply hurt and disappointed. I do not know what happened exactly, but Father came home one day complaining to Mother about how Mr. Ng passed sarcastic remarks about his tab. He wanted Father to settle all outstanding payment before making further purchases. To do this, Mother had to pawn some of her few remaining gold pieces. That incident left a strong impression on me as it taught me that the real world can be a cruel place. Nevertheless, Father continued to order things from the shop as he had treated Mr. Ng as a friend.

The kampung spirit

Our estate along Margaret Drive was a small one. There were only a few blocks of three- and four-storey flats. Our neighbours were mainly from other parts of the island, such as River Valley, Bukit Ho Swee, and outlying areas north of Singapore. Our direct community was made up mostly of Chinese families of various dialects —mostly Teochew, Hokkien, Cantonese, and Hakka — though there were also a few Indian families and one Eurasian family. As far as I can remember, our immediate Malay neighbours were those who stayed at the staff quarters next to my primary school. All my Malay classmates were from outside of our estate.

As the township was smaller then, neighbours knew each other well and the mood was especially cordial during festive seasons. It was common for neighbours to bake cakes or prepare food dishes and exchange them with each other during those occasions. When Lau Sim gave us *kueh nerng kor* or *yutou gao* (Chinese: 芋头糕, yam cake), Mother would return the favour by offering her homemade cake or even curry chicken. It was rare for us to buy cake from the market as most people usually prepared their own food.

Those were the days when a sense of kampung spirit or neighbourliness prevailed, something not so easily found today. Nowadays, most neighbours do not associate with one another as readily as before. We seldom practise courtesies such as inviting neighbours over for meals or exchanging food items. Maybe the stress of modern-day living and the stronger sense of competition, both at school and at work, is the cause. It seems like we have lost a part of our heritage and culture. There is also a sense that we are somewhat at a loss as to what to do with the abundant material wealth we have worked so hard to accumulate. Life was more basic than now but we were just as happy then if not more so. Perhaps simplicity brings with it a kind of joy.

Good and bad neighbours

The residents at the Blue Windows were generally nice and lived together in a close-knit community where everyone knew one another and even addressed each other with nicknames. "*Kuah ke*" was a term we often used. Nonetheless, it was also common for some neighbours to avoid crossing paths with one another. The reasons for this could range from petty jealousy or monetary matters, such as a failure to collect due for tontine. Tontine was a kind of illegal investment arrangement in which a group of people received high interest by lending their money to the highest bidder who wanted to secure the money as a loan.

My family did have a petty ongoing feud with the Hokkien family that lived above our flat. The conflict arose because of the leaking toilet from their unit. Although the conflict lasted till the day we moved out of the Blue Windows, in retrospect, it was unfortunate that we had gotten ourselves so upset over this matter. Our two families eventually became friends again years later. Another example of such hostile relationships was when the mother of my primary school teacher, Miss Toh, quarrelled with their next door neighbour, a housewife. They each accused the other of stealing clothing from their cloth lines. This sounds ridiculous, but their shouting and scolding resonated throughout the neighbourhood and their animosity was the talk among neighbours for quite a while. They even fought over the pet dog that my teacher kept. At one point, the police were even called in to resolve their conflict. Luckily, the men usually left the quarrels to the women and continued reading their newspaper or playing mahjong.

A neighbour who intrigued us was a taciturn, middle-aged man. He had lost one of his arms for reasons unknown to us. He lived opposite my block of flats resided and looked like businessman to me, though I really did not have the slightest idea of what he did for a living. He stayed with his wife and a few children, but they too were quite reserved and kept to themselves most of the time. This meant that no one we knew was familiar with him or his family members. Since his flat, also on the first floor of their block, was quite a distance from ours, there were few chances for us to cross paths. Once a month, however, this man would use his film projector to screen open-air silent movies for all the neighbours to enjoy. When he hung a piece of white cloth on his balcony, the neighbours would know immediately that he was going to indulge us with free movie that evening.

A group of children and some adults, mostly old aunties and uncles, would gather below his flat to see the movie for 30 minutes to an hour or so. Since our flat faced his directly, my family had the luxury of watching the show from our balcony. I cannot recall what movies he screened for us, but they were mostly adventure films about cowboys, and occasionally cartoons such as *Popeye the Sailorman*. What was amazing was that he did all this for free. It was certainly a good example of the community spirit that existed at that time. Many residents were initially interested in and excited at the prospect of the free shows. But after black-and-white televisions appeared in everyone's own home, the open air movies came to a sudden halt and yet another old way of life at the Blue Windows faded away.

Work

Most of our neighbours who lived at the Blue Windows were regular, working-class people. The community as a whole was not considered poor, and people were mostly employed in a variety of ordinary occupations such as teachers, cashiers, and hawkers.

Having been English-educated, Father worked as a cashier in the sales department of Sime Darby for his whole life till his retirement in 1975. His desk-bound work was a junior position that required him to be in the office till late evening. His salary was a mere 500 dollars and somehow had to feed a family of more than ten. I admired Father's ability to calculate large sums of money easily; at that time, even electronic calculators were unheard of. Although the staff in Father's office had a mechanical note-counting machine, most companies, especially small and medium-sized family businesses, used the abacus. However, Father often lamented that his job of counting money was tedious and monotonous. He had to balance the accounts at the end of each working day; unfortunately, he had to make up for any shortage with his own money and return any excess for the purposes of "accountability". Because of this, he openly discouraged his children from taking up jobs that involved handling large sums of cash. Perhaps this is why none of us ended up in the financial sector.

To supplement his income, Father became a part-time interpreter. He had tried giving tuition earlier but it had not gone well. The interpretation assignments were often given to him by his brother-in-law, my mother's sister's husband. Uncle Yeo (杨姑丈) was a Chinese primary school principal while my aunt was working as a Chinese primary school teacher. Since both the husband and wife were working, I knew that they were much better off than us financially. Besides, they only had four children compared to my parents, who had eight. Nevertheless, my father worked hard to provide for all of us and commanded a lot of respect from those who knew him. The brothers-in-law had a good relationship with each other. About once a month, Father and Mother would bring us children to their flat in the Newton area. During such visits, Father, being a good cook, would very often help to prepare the sumptuous dinner while my brothers and I would play with our cousins at the open field next to their flat.

Mother was a housewife who had to look after eight children. Luckily she had help from Grandma and Small Aunt. Even then, Mother made tiny baby shoes out of coloured cloth, which was then sold by one of Father's close friends. This enterprise helped bring in some extra income for the family. When my elder brother completed his secondary school education, Father got him a job as a salesman at Sime Darby. He first sold Campbell soup and performed poorly. He was later assigned to do direct sales of Electrolux vacuum cleaners. He did so well there that he eventually bought a brand new Ford.

Another Uncle Yeo (杨叔), one of my father's friends who was about the same age as him, was one of the few businessmen in our estate. He sold wrist watches for a living and had a shop downtown and so we nicknamed him "The Watch Uncle" (手表叔) in our Teochew dialect. Father sometimes went over to his house after dinner to chit-chat. Mother and a few of us children would tag along on some of these visits, but it was usually Father who stayed on to talk about current affairs and politics. I did not really like to follow Father on such visits for a simple reason: one of Uncle Yeo's daughters happened to be my Primary One classmate. Her results were much better than mine and I did not like it when our parents inevitably compared our results. Besides, my siblings liked to tease me by saying that she was my girlfriend, which was clearly not true! Such simple friendships could easily last a lifetime: my father and Uncle Yeo kept in touch even after both families moved to different parts of Singapore in the late 1970s.

One of our closest neighbours was another uncle we addressed as "Lau Chek" (老叔) for he was much older, at that time into his 70s, and a retiree. He lived next to our block. His attire was very special too: he usually put on homemade, long white trousers with a black belt tied around his waist and a white singlet to match. He also liked to smoke *ang hoong* (Hokkien: 红烟, red cigarette) —

raw tobacco wrapped in thin white paper. Father was also a smoker, but he smoked branded cigarettes such as 555 and Peter Stuyvesant. It was a free market in those days and there were no restrictions on cigarette advertisements. In fact, it was customary for families to provide cigarettes, contained in round metal tins, and match boxes during occasions such as weddings or funeral wakes.

Lau Chek, surnamed "Heng", sometimes brought along a few other neigbours when he visited us at our flat, usually in the evening. On these occasions, Mother would often prepare egg porridge for supper for the visitors and all the children. I fondly remember Mother simply boiling some white rice and adding in a fresh egg, some dried shrimps and sauces, and topping off each bowl of porridge with fried onions. It tasted delicious.

Lau Chek and the neighbours would talk about current affairs and politics. Father was a soft-spoken and gentle man who seldom made his stand known, especially on matters concerning local politics. He was more a listener than a participant in such discussions. Lau Chek, however, was so passionate about in politics — whether local or international — that discussions with him were often intense; voices would be raised and the sound of him rapping his knuckles on the tables could be heard. However, others quickly learnt not to take his aggression personally as he tended to get worked up and emotional when discussing politics. We were at first puzzled by the adults' behavior but eventually got used to such scenes, which were often replayed in the living room of our tiny flat.

One of Lau Chek's adult sons worked as a pirate taxi driver while the younger one worked as an odd-job labourer. The younger son, being closer in age to my elder brother, would sometimes visit us and chit chat with my brothers. At that time, reading Chinese kung-fu comic books was a trend among young people and became one of the main topics of discussion among them. Lau Chek also had a daughter we called Mei Ko (妹姑, Sister Aunt) who was very close to my Small Aunt. The two of them were very close friends and remained so even into old age. Mei Ko was an outgoing and talkative girl who was around my Small Aunt's age. There was always laughter when she came over as she liked to joke around and tease us. She worked as a seamstress and was therefore very particular about fashion, often offering advice to my elder brother on how to dress up smartly as a young man.

We children called the head of that family "Gao Chek" (Teochew: 九叔, ninth uncle) and his wife "Gao Sim" (Teochew: 九婶, ninth aunt). They were Teochew like us and my parents got to know them well through frequent visits. Like us, the family had quite a number of children. Gao Chek was a hawker who sold Teochew *poong tor kueh*. As far as I can remember, Gao Sim was very critical of her husband, whom she deemed lazy and unproductive. She would complain about his many bad habits to my grandmother and mother; women in those days liked to engross themselves in sorting out these domestic problems. Gao Chek's mother was an elderly woman who was also my Grandma's friend. Quite often, the two grandmothers would get together and bring along their respective grandchildren to wayang shows during Chinese festivals and other Taoist celebrations and prayer sessions.

CHAPTER 4

SCHOOL LIFE IN THE 60s AND 70s

Strathmore Primary School

Like most Singaporeans, I began my formal education at the age of seven. My parents enrolled me in Strathmore Primary School and I was the first child in the family to attend an English medium school. Strathmore Primary School was one of the three schools behind our block of flats and was next to the big canal. The other two schools were Queenstown Primary School and Birkhall Primary School. The school was just a stone's throw away from home. In fact, the only thing that separated my flat and the school's driveway was a chain-link fence. Indeed, we could see the classrooms of my school from the kitchen windows of our flat. Beyond the main school building was a big sports field.

Like most schools in those early years, my primary school also had quarters for its staff within the compound. At that time, schools did not have an automated bell and the end of each period was signaled by a school attendant, who had to go and ring the school bell manually. This staff quarters consisted of a block of three-storey flats next to the main building, with two units on each floor. It was occupied by my school's Malay cleaners and attendants and their families.

In the classrooms, teachers used to write on a blackboard with white and occasionally coloured chalk. The

The three-storey Strathmore Primary School servants' quarters in the 1960s, on the right of the school's main building. (Photo by author's father)

whiteboard was not widely adopted until the 1990s. A duster was used to clear the blackboard. During those days, some teachers would resort to throwing chalk or dusters at students who misbehaved or slept in class. When students misbehaved, teachers would say, "Don't behave like those Bukit Ho Swee *chang cheng kia* (Teochew: "sam seng", Malay for "gangster"). Everyone knew of the Bukit Ho Swee area as a place with a lot of gangsters and secret society members.

It was uncommon then for parents to lodge complaints against the teachers for doing so. Parents were actually grateful to teachers for disciplining their children. Sad to say, if such a practice were to occur in schools now, the teacher in question would probably lose his or her job or face even worse consequences. No wonder most people of my generation agree that students of yesteryear were a much better lot in terms of discipline and showing respect to one's elders.

The vice principal of my school was Mr. Goh, coincidently a close relative of my uncle's wife. He was also the discipline master and was a stern, no-nonsense man. We were all very scared of him. I cannot recall the name of the principal, but I remember my first form teacher, a quiet and soft-spoken lady whose husband was a medical doctor working for a government clinic. Her husband was once sent to my school to conduct a medical checkup for students and on that day, she acted as his "nurse" by getting her students to go for the checkup.

A regular day at school

Every morning, Grandma would walk me and my younger brother and sister to school, even though it was just a stone's throw away. During my first few years in that school, I did not get any pocket money for recess from my parents. Instead, during recess, my mother or grandmother would pass our meals through the gate of the chain-link fence for my younger brother, my younger sister and me. Sometimes, Mother would even bring the meals to the school canteen, then known to us as the "tuck shop".

My school had two sessions then. Around noon, when the morning session ended and the afternoon session was about to begin, a lot of students, parents, and grandparents would mill around the schools and my flat. Unlike today, domestic helpers did not form part of this crowd as it was uncommon for families to hire them then. A pushcart would be just around the corner and the uncle ran a brisk business selling homemade ice cream. He would be shaking a handheld bell to alert customers of his presence and the "ring ring" sound was something we were familiar with growing up.

When we were younger, Grandma walked us back from school but as we grew up, my younger sister and brother and I went home alone. After all, we simply had to walk through the gate of the chain-link fence. It was routine for us to have lunch at home with our mother before "homework time". At 3 o'clock sharp, it would be "break time" and my mother would give us some titbits, usually homemade snacks such as sweet potato *kueh*. Small Aunt would start to prepare for dinner by cooking rice at around 4 o'clock.

On some days, I would visit my school friends after I finished my homework. One of them was an Indian-Muslim friend by the name of Ali. He stayed with his family and fireman father in the government fire station quarters at Stirling Road, a short distance from my Margaret Drive flat. Very often after school, we would go and watch the Malay boys in the nearby field play football.

Another schoolmate I remember is Chee Kiong. He was a classmate of mine in Primary Four. Most of my classmates did not like to play with Chee Kiong as he was a reserved boy. He had an unsmiling face and a frail and dark, small-framed body. His hair was always unkempt, but he was always neatly dressed in his school uniform. In the words of our teacher, he was a "weak student", though his results were actually better than mine. Though I am not sure why I felt that way, I remember sensing a certain sadness in Chee Kiong. His father worked as a building contractor. Despite his quiet demeanor, Chee Kiong was very proud of this fact and liked to tell all his friends that his father was the contractor for the church along Queensway.

Significant Primary School events

Some of the interesting events that occurred in my first primary school included Sports Day, National Day, and the time just after the end of PSLE (Primary School Leaving Exam) when my school became the designated centre for the marking of examination scripts.

For Sports Day, students were given free Milo or Ovaltine. I did not participate in any sport then and was a mere spectator. Indeed, we could even watch the games from our kitchen window. My parents were delighted when my younger brother won a prize for a running event during the 1966 Sports Day. My younger sister also participated in a relay running event in the same year but did not win anything; my father praised her for her effort nonetheless.

A few days before National Day, teachers and attendants of my school would put up decorations such as flags and colourful banners in front of the school. The other two neighbouring schools did the same thing. Inevitably, there would be some form of friendly competition among the three schools to outdo one another and be the most beautifully decorated school. On the eve of National Day, the school would hold a Speech and Prize-giving Day when every student would receive a souvenir. Those who had done well were given book prizes. Despite my poor academic performance, my teacher had a good impression of me as I was very well-behaved and unassuming. For that, I was awarded a Good Conduct prize when I was in Primary Four. The prize was an Oxford English Dictionary, which I have kept to this day.

After the end of the PSLE, a three-day holiday was declared to enable teachers from all over Singapore to mark the scripts. As my school was designated by the Ministry of Education as a centre for marking examination scripts, cars belonging to teachers would be parked along the long driveway leading to the school. The holiday also meant that students were free to stay at home and watch TV or play ball games.

Faring badly in primary school

Being the first child in the family to attend an English medium school, I was at a total loss in school. Not many parents could afford to send their children to kindergarten in those days and mine were no exception. English was totally foreign to me. At home, we spoke in the Teochew dialect. My two older brothers and Small Aunt were all from Chinese-medium schools. Although my father could speak and write good English (he completed three years of English-medium secondary school at Stamford School after his early Chinese education at Tuan Mong Primary School), he was too busy to teach me. Furthermore, he hardly spoke to me in English at home.

Not surprisingly, my early years of schooling were difficult. After Primary One, I was always among the worst students in my class. My inability to do well in school was a great disappointment to my parents. My natural aversion to learning English, a language I considered strange, during my childhood days did not help the situation. Despite their efforts at getting me to go for tuition and a constant barrage of warnings from both my teachers and my parents, I continued to fail miserably.

My siblings, however, all did well in school. Perhaps that was why I was reserved in school but stubborn and rebellious at home. It was my Grandma who supported me — despite my bad behaviour at home and poor performance in school — with equal stubbornness, telling everyone that although this grandson of hers was slow in school, she knew beyond a doubt that he would one day become a good businessman, just like his great-grandfather. He is said to have owned acres and acres of rubber plantation in Malaya and Indonesia. I am not sure what gave her that impression but I knew that, although she loved all her grandchildren, she gave me more attention than the rest.

Despite her supportive presence, I still disliked examinations and had an intense fear of receiving my report card before school closed for the year-end holiday. The end of each year brought with it the much-dreaded tests and examinations. Father tried his best to teach me, but I somehow failed to register anything. In the end, he gave up and engaged a tutor to help me with my school work. The lady tutor, Ms. Goh, also stayed along Margaret Drive. In fact, her flat was next to the then Queenstown Prison. The vicinity of her flat was quiet and dimly lit. Worse still, the narrow road that led to her house was not lit up at all. It was indeed a challenge for me to go to her flat for tuition as I had to walk back home in near-total darkness after. I used to be so scared that I would hold on to my books tightly and run back home the moment I left the lady tutor's house.

That was just the beginning of troubles that arose from my poor results. When I was in Primary Six, I received my first slap from Mr Singh, a teacher of mine. Mr Singh was a big and stern middle-aged man who, like many Sikh men during those days, wore a turban on his head and spotted a long beard. A few days after an examination, he slapped me hard on the right side of my face, hitting my right ear. I had failed my second term examination again, even after a poor showing in the first term.

Things got worse when my face started to swell. Going home that day must have been one of the worst times of my childhood: I brought with me a report card full of red marks, a swollen face marked with the imprint of my teacher's palm, a right ear that was bright red, and a deep sense of failure. Furthermore, I started to hear a ringing sound in my ear.

The first person I went to was my mother. Luckily, she was sympathetic toward me, although she also knew that my teacher probably meant well. Still, she thought he had no right to slap me with so much force and without a proper explanation. In Teochew, she told me that we would go to see both a government doctor and Mr Singh the next day. Despite my protests — I was terrified of him — she spoke to my dad about it and insisted on going.

We arrived at the teachers' common room before assembly the next morning and Mother went directly to Mr Singh, who was seated at his desk next to the window. As my mother complained, Mr Singh tried to justify himself: I had been very inattentive, I was not doing my best, he had put in a lot of effort to no avail, the other boys were not like me, my brother was so much better than me, etc. Although he did not use the word "stupid", it was clear through his actions and expressions that he thought I was "stupid". Still, my mother insisted, these reasons did not justify the use of such force.

Mr Singh started to look worried. My mother finally threatened to go see the principal if he did it again and walked off abruptly. Left alone in the company of Mr Singh, I felt intimidated and confused! My instinct was to run back to my classroom but he called out my name. He explained that he slapped me because he wanted me to come to my senses, he did not mean to hurt me. A new sense of security came over me and I apologised for my mother's confrontation. Mr Singh looked tired and was quiet for a while. Then he gently patted me on my shoulder, told me to get ready for class and to try doing better in tests the next time. Desperate to get out of the awkward situation, I nodded my head eagerly and promised to do so.

From then on, Mr Singh never used physical force on me or any of the other students. We grew to be less fearful of him. Unfortunately, my poor academic results continued. Equally unfortunate was the fact that this was not the only time I would get slapped in the course of my formal education.

Jervois West Primary School

As fate would have it, I failed the Primary School Leaving Examination (PSLE). This turned out to be a blessing in disguise. My first school did not accept retainee students like myself who had failed the PSLE and so I was transferred to another school along Jervois Road. This was a small integrated primary school with both English and Malay as the mediums of instruction. Because the school was further away from my house, I woke up early in the morning and often hitched a ride on the back of a lorry belonging to my classmate's father. A few of my other classmates who also stayed at the Blue Windows went with me.

My life changed after that early setback as I suddenly realized the importance of doing well in school. Thus began my struggle to get back on my feet. Jervois West was unlike my previous school in many ways. The first thing I noticed about the school was its badly maintained building. It looked so much older than my first school, and this dampened my mood further. Adding to my grievances must have been the realization that most of my friends were probably in bigger and nicer secondary schools while I was trapped in this gloomy, rundown place! I later found out that Jervois West was a "dumping ground" for students like me from neighbouring schools who had failed the PSLE.

In spite of its bad reputation, Jervois West Primary School offered students a more conducive learning environment. Unexpectedly, it was there that I got a chance to experience one of the most amazing sights in my life: a magical white mist.

I experienced this view nearly every day on the open school field — no smaller than the one in my first school — that was surrounded by rows of mature Angsana trees and flowering plants. The school's location at the high-end residential area of Tanglin contributed to its lush greenery and serene setting. I will long cherish the feeling of freshness and jubilation that I experienced each morning on entering the school's main gate on Jervois Road. The thick and heavy white mist that seemed to be floating lightly on the open field was the first thing that greeted me when I walked past the field. In fact, I intentionally reached the school earlier just so I could run into the foggy mist and immerse myself into the fast disappearing white mist. I loved it! It was like floating with the clouds! The joy of being amidst nature, albeit just for a brief moment, is something I will never forget. However, all students had to sing the national anthem in front of the school main building at 7:30 in the morning and I would rush back to join in the ceremony.

Our form teacher, Mr. Lee, was a serious-looking, young, bespectacled man who was extremely dedicated to helping his students. He taught us Mathematics and English. He would even conduct extra classes on Saturdays just to ensure that students like me did not miss the chance to get promoted to secondary school. Compared to my teachers at the previous school, the teachers at Jervois West were always helpful and friendly. Arrogance had no place among teachers and students; only hard work and camaraderie. There, the teachers understood that their

The Jervois West Integrated Primary School building in 2011. It was used by the Singapore School of the Deaf and then vacated in 2007.

students were simply slow learners who had yet to develop their potential for learning. They took pains to guide us, encourage us, and provide us with opportunities to excel. I learnt more in the brief year I was enrolled there than the six years I spent in my former school. The experience also inspired me tremendously when I myself became a teacher at the Singapore Polytechnic. I tried to emulate my teachers' patience, understanding, and forgiveness.

Gradually I grew to like my second school, its teachers and my new classmates, many if not all of whom were repeat students. Most were from poor families; some were reserved like me, and naturally, a number of them were loud and unruly. Notwithstanding such a diverse mix of pupils, most made a real effort to pass the year-end examination. Time flew by and soon it was time for the PSLE again. This time round, I was fortunate to pass the examination and go on to secondary school. I was and remain grateful for Mr. Lee's guidance and effort. Without his assistance, I would not have been able to progress academically.

Kim Seng Technical School

I was posted to Kim Seng Technical School, located along Kim Seng Road, after the PSLE was over. My ideal school was Victoria School, but my results were nowhere near the marks required for admission there. Nevertheless, I would spend the next four happy years of my education at Kim Seng Technical. Being one of the earliest technical schools in Singapore, it was an integrated school with both English and Chinese streams. Even then, there was very little inter-action between the students of the two streams, something I consider one of the limitations of the school policy at that time. Moreover, despite having a Chinese stream, not much emphasis was placed on learning Mandarin. This is a failure that I deeply regretted in my later life as the language has turned out to be very important with the emergence of China.

Opposite the school was the then famous Great World Amusement Centre. As students, we liked to loiter there after class. The entire area contained a Chinese empo-rium, a rather sizeable aquarium and a Chinese restaurant. School in those days was definitely less stressful than it is now. As students, we had the luxury of play and interac-tion among ourselves and strong friendships were fostered in that time. Those years must have been one of my happiest times so far.

When I was in Secondary Three, I was hospitalized at the then Outram Road General Hospital, now Singa-pore General Hospital, for a minor operation on my right ear. I was warded in Bowyer Block, the building with the imposing clock tower that still stands today. It is no longer in use but houses a hospital museum and functions as a walkway that links other blocks in the hospital. The conditions at the hospital then were quite shocking. The wards were crowded and cramped; patients had to make do with torn mattresses and blankets, and the lighting at night was dim. I actually had to sleep on a bed along the corridor leading to the ward. For two nights, I was horrified by the death of a few patients since nurses and attendants would push hospital beds with corpses on them pass my bed. I was so scared that I almost wanted to run home! Despite having to stay at the hospital for only three days, I was grateful that two of my classmates came to visit me at the hospital and was relieved when the doctor allowed me to return home.

In Secondary Three, I got slapped again. This time it was on the left side of my face after the flag-lowering ceremony in school in the evening. Again, I felt like I did not deserve what I got. By secondary school, I had toned down and was generally well-behaved. My only "error" was standing beside a bunch of mischievous boys who refused to sing the national anthem and were making noise and fooling around instead. The discipline master — a fierce man in his thirties —rushed to the back of the line where most of the noise was coming from. He had a tendency toward sudden outbursts of anger and was definitely a sight to behold when furious, with a red face and violent temper. Quickly, he proceeded to slap the faces of all the boys in close proximity. It was done quickly, within seconds, and with almost military precision. Wah! I had no idea what hit me at all!

Again, I told my mother what had happened once I got home. Being the caring woman that she is, she enquired if I was hurt. This time, she knew that I had been maligned; afterall I was very well-behaved in secondary school. I never got to explain myself or prove my innocence to the discipline master. It was clear to me that the slap was not justified. Neither was this mode of punishment justifiable, even if my classmates had been misbehaving. If he had done that now, there is no doubt that that man would have lost his job. He had the right to both be angry and discipline the students, but to resort to such a violent and sudden show of physical force is something no modern educator would advocate.

Unlike my primary school years, my academic career in secondary school was relatively smooth. We were poor then and unlike some of my classmates, I could not afford the luxury of tuition. Luckily, my parents found that I was a hardworking and self-motivated child. My school teachers were naturally pleased that I was such a keen learner. I had indeed put in extra effort in my school work and my father was spared from the worry that I would not make it to university. I had long made up my mind that I would do the best I could to earn a degree in time to come. What inspired me to do well was a determination to sacrifice the present for the future; "先我不享，后我为能" is a personal motto that has guided me since then. This time round, I would always be among the top few students in my class.

Our hobbies

Without electronic gadgets, it was imperative that people, especially children, were innovative when it came to leisure activities. Leisurely pursuits in the 1970s were simple and were either free or very cheap. Sports we engaged in included badminton and table tennis. A group of men from our estate would play badminton at the court right in front of the block of flats on most weekend evenings. Most children would play table tennis in schools or even on makeshift table tennis tables. Not surprisingly, we had never heard of squash, tennis, or golf.

One leisure activity that children no longer indulge in is catching spiders. Unlike in our present-day concrete jungle, spiders were abundant then. Schoolchildren then pit the spiders they caught against one another's to see who had the most aggressive and powerful spider. Money, usually a few cents, was quite often involved as well. At other times, strong spiders would even be put up for sale among the students. This was against the school rules but then again, all these activities were "undercover" and teachers usually turned a blind eye to such cases so long as no trouble was created.

School children either caught or bought fighting fish for the same purpose of pitting them against one another. The fish were kept in separate glass containers. A piece of cardboard or paper was put between the two containers to prevent the fish from seeing each other. They were so aggressive that they would keep charging against the glass containers if they did! When the fight began, the fish were released at the same time into a bigger tank to fight one another. A cruel and unpleasant act no doubt, but it was common practice back then and people seemed to accept it. The owner of the winning fish would stand a chance to win money from the loser. Bystanders on the other hand, could bet on which of the two fish would win the match. Unlike the fighting spiders, most of the fighting fish were owned by adults. Very often, these adults also indulged in collecting birds of various species. There were bird-singing competitions then, just like today.

Despite our general docility, fighting among school boys as a result of these activities or "staring incidents" was common and usually happened at English medium schools then. These were usually minor but a boy from my school was once stabbed in the stomach by another boy from a nearby school. The ambulance had to be summoned and our head master was furious that such an incident had happened in our school. As punishment, all the boys' except for those from the top class, were made to stay back in school for an extra hour the following day. At that time, it was commonly agreed that students from the Chinese medium schools were generally better behaved than those from English medium schools. This could be due to the fact that the curriculum in Chinese schools emphasized moral values and good behavior. I believe my primary school English textbooks, the Federal Readers Book One to Six, were more Western-oriented and comprised mostly fairytales and focused on the sciences. Chinese texts on the other hand were filled with stories that either high-lighted the need to respect one's parents and teachers or taught a certain moral lesson.

Another pastime of the people living at the Blue Windows was kite flying. Kites of various sizes but of limited variety were a common sight at some of the open spaces near our estate during the weekends. At that time, the estate was still not heavily built up and we could find such open spaces on Mei Ling Street or around Forfar House. As with fighting spiders, kite flying also created problems for parents and school teachers. Some of the more naughty children would coat their kite strings with glass powder to cut the strings of other kites as a kind of one-upmanship. Besides causing frequent arguments and fights, there were also reported cases of these glass-coated strings cutting unsuspecting peoples' necks. One had to be very careful in the presence of these kite flyers. Eventually, this practice was banned.

One of the simple games of the 1970s was *goli* (Malay: marbles). At that time, playing marbles was almost an essential skill among school boys. The ball-shaped, glass marbles came in various designs and colours. Grandma used to give us marbles wrapped in old newspapers each time she returned from the in-law's shop, known to us only as "Golden Hill"(金山) along North Bridge Road. The shopowner, who was my father's cousin, made plastic toys for children and was also a wholesaler of coloured marbles.

To make some extra pocket money, my two older brothers took on the enterprise of selling these marbles to their schoolmates. In addition, they also sold tiny plastic figure toys in the form of lions, tigers, horses and other animals. There were various ways to play *kuti-kuti* (Malay: *kutik*, to pick up). For example, you could use one of your fingers to hit your own plastic toy in such a way that it fell on top of your opponent's one. If you succeeded, you would have "eaten up" your opponent's animal and would then own that piece. Each person took turns to strike his or her opponent's pieces until one party lost all of his or her plastic toys. Of course, the more plastic figures you won or gathered, the more powerful your skills would have had to be. You could also convert some of your collection into cash by selling them off to friends for, say, five cents for ten pieces.

While my parents did not allow us to gamble, not even during the Chinese New Year, some of us boys would sometimes secretly go to a stationery shop near the wet market to try our luck at a game known as *"tikam-tikam"* (Malay: to choose randomly). Giving five cents to the aunty at the store entitled a customer to choose a piece of folded paper out of the small pile on the colourful cardboard sheet. If the number printed on that folded paper matched any number that came with a prize, the customer would win the prize that corresponded to the number. Otherwise, it was five cents down the drain. Prizes included fountain pens, plastic cameras, notebooks, and even wrist watches. As with all forms of gambling, the chances of winning were remote. Nevertheless, I played *tikam-tikam* after school on many occasions. Unfortunately, short of a few sweets that served as consolation prizes, I cannot remember winning a single decent prize. Because school children were forgoing food to play *tikam-tikam* games with their pocket money, hawkers were eventually banned from selling *tikam-tikam* to children.

While games such as those described above were common among the boys, girls had their own preferred games too. Understandably, their games were mostly played indoors and were less rigorous. Many girls enjoyed playing "Five Stones". Basically, this game involves throwing five small, hand-sewn pyramids — made of cloth and filled with uncooked rice, wheat or sand — into the air and trying to catch them. My sisters are probably in a better position to describe the rules since I had no interest in learning how to play what we boys considered a girl's game! Besides Five Stones, school girls also liked to play Hopscotch, a game in which one had to jump through rectangular spaces, drawn with chalk, without falling outside the boundaries. School girls drawing the Hopscotch grids on the concrete floor and hopping their time away while waiting for the school bell to ring was a common sight. Younger girls liked playing "*masak-masak*" (Malay: cooking) with plasticware and nicely dressed up dolls. These were made-in-China dolls, with eyes and lips that could open and close manually, very much like the dolls we have today.

My pen pal

Instead of Facebook, the young of yesteryear corresponded with their friends through snail mail. Young people at that time also made pen pals through newspapers and magazines. I myself made some friends in this way. During my secondary school days, I even had a pen pal girlfriend from Taiping, Malaysia. She was the first real female friend I had. Soon after our initial correspondence, I started to receive beautiful coloured photographs of her in her garden and other places of interests in Malaysia. I liked to look at those photographs and reread what she wrote. She enclosed her letters — written on soft, colourful paper and decorated with her drawings — in colourful and romantic-looking envelopes.

Iris was from a large Peranakan Chinese family and her father was a successful, no-nonsense businessman who dealt in tin mines and property. He was a rich man with a big family, a big house and many big cars. A photograph of Iris sitting in between a slim, middle-aged, fearsome-looking man and a kind-looking, petite woman attested to her characterization of him. Even to this day, I marvel at how unlike her dad she was. Luckily, Iris took after her mum more than her dad, she would not have been my pen pal otherwise! Despite the fact that her father was strict with all his children, he was a loving dad. Being the youngest, Iris was his favourite child. In one of her letters, she wrote very touching stories about how hard her dad worked to provide for her family — first as a labourer, then as a supervisor — before he struck it rich with his tin mining business. I was impressed by but also afraid of the man.

Like teenagers of today on Facebook, Iris and I continued to write to each other about our school life, our friends, and our likes and dislikes. We even wrote about our aspirations for the future. Unconsciously, we soon fell madly in love with each other. I was captivated by Iris's charm and pretty face and soon considered her the love of my life. For a long while I thought of her day and night, even when attending classes. My teachers and parents noticed that I was spending a lot of time at my desk, thinking that I was doing my homework when in fact I was romancing my newfound sweetheart! Luckily, I was clever enough to hide my thoughts from them and they did not find any other discernable change in my behavior. Slowly, we progressed to pour out our admiration and affection for each other. We both harboured hopes of meeting up with each other and eventually becoming partners in life. Yet, such a shallow romance was hard to sustain for long, especially if two persons were as young, naïve and far apart as we were then.

Not surprisingly, this sweet exchange of letters came to sudden halt. One gloomy afternoon, while anxiously waiting for the postman to deliver letters to our flat, I received her missive. In that last letter, she wrote:

Dear Kyang,

I am sad to tell you that my parents had come to know about our distant relationship and are very angry with me for spending time writing to you and not studying! Just to let you know that Pa was very angry that my exam results have been badly affected. I was no longer in the top three positions in my class. I only managed [to get] number twenty. It came as a shock to them and a setback to me. It is not your fault though, for I am to blame for not studying hard enough.

Because of this, Pa has confiscated and burned all the letters you sent me last Friday afternoon. It pained me to see them in flames and in smoke. I could not do anything about it, except to cry my heart out. Not only that, Pa wanted me to stop writing to you immediately and not to have anything to do with you. It is nothing personal I assure you. For he himself told Mum that you look decent and must be a good boy. But to them, we are too young to think of BG [Boy-Girl] relationship. How old fashioned of them? It was with my pitiful crying, my persistent begging and with Mum's timely pleading, that he finally allowed me to write you this last letter.

Kyang, Pa has arranged for me to stay with his older sister in Penang and I do not know for how long! I will be with my mum in Penang by the time this letter reaches you. Aunty is a good tutor and Pa was sure [that] Aunty will help me catch up with my school work and hopefully, I should be in the top of my class again next term. He takes this very, very seriously as he had plans to send me to medical school in UK and be a good doctor in future.

I know you will be sad to hear all this and maybe you will also be angry with me for agreeing to go. I have no choice and no means to resist as an order from Pa is an order not to be disobeyed. Hope you understand my hard situation.

But, do stay strong and as all things, good or bad, must come to an end, let ours end here with mutual warm feeling. Kyang, I have to tell you that I am still very sad and I know you are just as sad, but I hope you should be strong and concentrate on your studies. Maybe, one day we shall meet again, if not here in Taiping, then maybe in Singapore. I just want to let you know that you will forever be in my heart. My thoughts go with you always and I hope you will at least remember me. But, even if you were to forget about me, I will still remember you. All I want is for you to be happy and have a good future.

Lastly, please do not worry too much about me and also do not bother to write me for now, as I will be away from home and your letter will not get to me anyway!

Good Bye and Good Luck.

Yours sincerely,
Iris
21 November 1970

I was heartbroken and disappointed for a few weeks after receiving this letter. Over the next two months, I sent her ten letters but they all went unanswered; in any case, she had already advised me not to contact her. In my last letter to her, I wrote:

Dear Iris,

The wind was blowing loudly and strongly outside the blue windows. The sky was filled with dark clouds as the unforgiving raindrops were falling on me as I read your letter, not once but many times, with tears in my eyes and needles in my heart.

I am very sad and very disappointed but I am not angry with you, not with your caring and lovely ways. I do understand your hard situation and I do understand why your Pa and Ma acted in that manner. Cruel as it may be, but I think they meant you good, my dear girl. Please do not make them angry again and respect them always. But, I shall think of you always and shall wait for you. I assure you I will, my dear Iris, for you are to me what a sail is to a boat.

Please Iris, please permit me to write to you again to explain to you and if needed to your parents. Just let me know where in Penang I can send my next letter to you. I have to, if not, I will be sad and desperate forever for losing you my dear.

Iris, I cannot hide from you that I am at a loss right now and I am crying my heart out too. But, do take care of yourself and remember that I will remember you forever and ever, no matter what happens to you and to me. Perhaps, someday somewhere we shall meet again and I hope the sooner the better. I wish you all the best in your studies. Take care.

> Yours sincerely,
> Kyang
> 28th November 1970

One practical thing I gained from this relationship was a better understanding of the geography of Malaysia! While it was possible for pen pals to eventually become lovers and then life partners, in most cases no face-to-face contact was made and long-term relationships seldom materialized. Communication was carried out solely by post. It certainly was a very romantic feeling to write a letter to a loved one and receive one in return. Nothing can replace love and tenderness expressed in the words of one's loved one in his or her own handwriting. Very often, even the paper on which the letter was written was specially supplemented with drawings and colourful designs. It was also exciting to wait anxiously for the postman to deliver that love letter to your doorstep. Such experiences surely bring back sweet memories of the past.

Sadly, writing and waiting to receive letters from loved ones has died a certain death in the computer age. In its place, we have emails and SMS. Gone were the days when seeing Mr. Postman coming to our house was a source of excitement and joy. Now, it has mainly become a source of stress, especially since what we now receive are mostly bills from credit card companies, other service providers and tax payable!

The GCE 'O' level examination

I was in the first batch of Secondary Four students to take the General Certification of Education (GCE) 'O' Level examinations instead of the University of Cambridge Secondary Four Leaving Examination in 1971. With the GCE 'O' Level, there was no classification as to whether a student achieved a "1", the best grade, or a "4", the worst. The number of 'O' Level passes or passes with distinction that each student obtained was recorded instead and the results published in all the four official-language newspapers.

"Good" schools with an established record of producing students with outstanding results in the Cambridge School Leaving Examinations were expected to replicate their success with the 'O' Levels. Indeed most of their students scored eight or more 'O' Level passes with distinctions. It is important to note that students' stress levels in the early 1970s cannot compare to our present-day levels since there was less competition, at least not from talented foreign students (there were hardly any of them at that time). I managed to do quite well in the 'O' Levels and continued my 'A' Level education at Queenstown Secondary Technical School.

The National Cash Registers (NCR) and the F&N factory

After taking our "O" Levels, the graduating students of Kim Seng got the opportunity to go on different post-exam excursions organized by our teachers. My class was assigned a visit to both the then National Cash Registers (NCR) at Havelock Road and the Fraser and Neaves (F&N) factory along River Valley Road. Both visits were fascinating.

At the NCR, we got to see big boxes of what, at that time, must have been the early beginnings of our modern computer age. Our present computer units are getting smaller and smaller; from the desktop to the laptop to the netbook to the iPad and the smartphone. Then, a computer took up the space of a classroom! Yet, the capacity of that system must have been negligible compared to what we can pack into a microSD card today. There was no such thing as hard disks, thumb drives or even floppy disks. What we saw instead were many drums in the computer module, which were the size of metal cabinets. I have no idea how it was executed but punch cards were used to enter data into the system. At that time, one of the NCR's objectives in arranging for students to visit their premises was to encourage them to go into the "computer industry". In 1973, the term "Information Technology" or "IT" had not been coined yet.

The visit to the F&N factory was also an eye-opening for most of us. Soft drinks, such as the carbonated orange-flavoured drinks, were sold in glass bottles instead of the metal cans or plastic bottles we use nowadays. Students always managed to get free drinks during those visits. Perhaps it was the visit to the factory that prompted my professional interest in noise issues. The whole time I was there I kept wondering, "How did the operators endure working in such a noisy environment?" At that time, not much emphasis was placed on the workers' health; safety and welfare issues were mostly ignored. I doubt that anyone put on hearing protectors or took precautions against hearing loss while working at the plant.

CHAPTER 5

CUSTOMS AND FESTIVALS

"Red" and "white" occasions

Life was simple during the 1960s. While the standard of living cannot be compared to what we have today, festive seasons such as Chinese New Year, Christmas, Hari Raya Puasa, and Deepavali certainly seemed much more fun then. The Chinese traditionally referred to these religious celebrations, as well as weddings, birthdays and other happy occasions, as "Red Events or Occasions" (红事). On the other hand, death among family members or relatives was usually referred to as "White Events or Occasions" (白事). Understandably, it was customary for red to be used for dressing and decorations for "Red Occasions" while black or white was used for "White Occasions".

Women in my household liked to make *kueh nerng kor* during festive occasions. These delicious yellow cakes were used as offerings to the gods or ancestors during prayers. Unlike the fresh cream cakes we have today, the ingredients used were simply flour, sugar and of course, fresh eggs. More well-off families could afford to use more eggs for each cake. Also, forget about the powerful electric whisks, we made do with a spring wire egg beater to beat the eggs manually. This device can still be seen today, although not many people use it nowadays. The well-mixed ingredients are then poured into a big bowl that is in turn placed in a hot, water-filled wok and steamed. The signature aspect is the cake's "topping": five red "imprints" each consisting of five tidy dots arranged in the form of a star. As children, we liked to volunteer for this task. We first dipped the end of the stick into red food colouring and then pressed the stick with five sharp pins against the freshly baked cake to form the pattern. If we were not careful, we would sometimes smear the colouring onto the cake and spoil it; this ensured us a stern scolding from Grandma.

Before major festive occasions, Mother would go to Chinatown to buy foodstuff. She brought along two or three of the children with her. The older siblings would help look after the younger ones during such trips. We had no car and a pirate taxi was too costly. so we went downtown on the No. 9 Hock Lee bus instead. I enjoyed taking the bus because I was fascinated by them, having seen pictures of buses in the textbooks in school and read about the going to town with mum and dad. Then, the children's stories in our English textbooks were simple and short, and there was none of the science fiction or fantasy that is so common today. By today's standards, fares were low. If I recall correctly, the entire trip was only five cents for children and perhaps ten cents for adults. The trip probably took half an hour and ended at the bus stop in front of the Majestic Theatre and the Nam Tien Hotel. Roads were less congested during those days and there was no expressway for speedier travel.

Chinatown (牛车水), pronounced as "Gu Chia Swee" in Hokkien and "Ngau Chay Sui" in Cantonese, was already a busy place then. Like now, it was the gathering place for Chinese people. There was a large Cantonese community

Mother and Small Aunt on Chinese New Year day in the 1960s.

residing there. Being well-versed in Cantonese, my mother had no trouble communicating with the vendors there. Occasionally, my mother would also take us to the afternoon Chinese movie screenings at the Majestic Theatre. As it is now, Chinatown was especially significant during the Chinese New Year period. Despite the fact that there was no large-scale lighting up of the area in the 1960s and 1970s, in my opinion, the festive mood then was much more authentic and joyful than it is now.

Chinese New Year

The Chinese consider *Chun Jie* (Chinese: 春节, Spring Festival) the beginning of the New Year and it means a fresh start for most people. Even thinking of the festival reminds me of things such as the *Ang Sai* (Hokkien: 红狮, Red Lion) orange soft drink, which was sold in glass bottles packed F&N. Unlike now, it was only during major events such as Chinese New Year or weddings that we got a taste of

Traditional Chinese New Year items such as a pair of mandarin oranges, cookies, greeting cards and an antique cast iron hexagonal small box on our new formica dining table. On the left is a transistor radio with an extended antennae.

soft drinks. Strangely enough, the *Ang Sai* orange and Sarsi favoured drinks were reserved for happy occasions while the Green Spot (绿宝) orange soft drink sold in smaller glass bottles were typically consumed during funerals.

Indeed, much of the fun of Chinese New Year occurred during the few weeks of preparation before the actual day. It was a time of great joy for children like us, especially when Uncle, an electrician, fixed up decorative lighting at the balcony. Flickering light bulbs of all colours were already available back then. We were proud to be one of the few households who had such decorations. Another of my most treasured memories must have been coming home from school to the smell of freshly baked Chinese New Year goodies such as "love letters", *kueh bangkit,* and steamed egg cakes. Mother and Grandma, together with

Our balcony, filled with Grandma's potted plants. During my uncle's wedding, it was furnished with decorative lights and a loudspeaker. A red cloth banner was also hung up to usher good luck and happiness into the home.

the help of Small Aunt, would be busy preparing such goodies for the festivities. We ate some of them while the rest were presented as gifts for neighbours, relatives, and friends. The cookies were also used as offerings to the various Taoist gods that my family worshipped in those days. Although as a child I could hardly comprehend what the adults were doing, my grandmother was in charge of the prayers and the entire family would follow her instructions without question.

My mother and three younger sisters making "love letters" for Chinese New Year in the early 1970s.

Of course, one of the best things about Chinese New Year is the food. My father and uncle were good cooks and although they were too busy to cook for the family on a daily basis, they often did the cooking during the Chinese New Year period. On the eve of Chinese New Year, the brothers would spend the whole afternoon in the small kitchen preparing dishes for the Reunion Dinner, the most important meal of the year. My uncle's specialty was sweet and sour fish while my father prepared most of the other dishes. At other times, most families just made do with simple and cheap meals. Unlike the countless food courts we have now, we had at best a few stalls selling noodles near our house. It was also difficult to find obese children during that period because most of the families could barely afford to provide their children with good food, much less fatten them up.

After dinner, my mother and sisters would clear up and prepare to welcome the God of Wealth (财神爷) at midnight. That was also when the firecrackers were lit. Of course, the memory of playing with firecrackers never fails to surface in the minds of people who grew up in the good old days. The firecrackers were most intense on the eve and the fifteenth day of the Chinese New Year. It was customary for neighbours to compete among themselves to see which family fired the most crackers and fireworks. The resultant noise would last for about an hour into the early morning of the New Year. A common sight the morning after a round of fireworks was set off was the front of flats covered with a thick layer of red paper residue. In fact, we believed that the thicker the layer of red debris, the more they welcomed the God of Wealth, who would then be more inclined to bestow the household with prosperity that year.

The next morning on the first day of the Chinese New Year, the whole family would gather for a vegetarian breakfast before we were allowed to consume any meat. As children, the first thing we had to do upon waking was to greet our grandmother, parents and older relatives, and wish them good health and good luck for the New Year. In turn, they would return our greetings and give us their blessing to do well in school.

Like most families, we children were very excited and looked forward to the first day of Chinese New Year. It meant two things for us: new clothes to put on and *angpow* (Hokkien: 红包, red packets) to receive from parents and relatives. When I was in Secondary One, I asked my parents for a pair of new leather shoes as most of my friends already had one. A few weeks before the New Year, my mother gave me five dollars, a princely sum then, so that I could get a pair. I was delighted and wore them to a New Year gathering with my friends. She even instructed me to get them from a shop in North Bridge Road. That

My younger brother and three sisters with me at the center. This was taken at Margaret Drive during Chinese New Year in 1968.

shop, known as Ching Ho, specialized in leather shoes and was where Father used to buy his own shoes.

Although the amount in the *angpow* was small, just a couple of dollars at most, I was always pleased with whatever I received from my parents. After all, my regular pocket money for school was just a few cents. The money we received was just enough for us to buy firecrackers and titbits; we were more than satisfied with that and dared not ask for more. When I received *angpow* from my relatives, I obediently handed them back to my parents. In turn, my parents would pack the same amount of money back into an *angpow* and give it to our relatives' children. With the low salary that my father earned as a cashier in Sime Darby, he could barely afford to give any money away. It was also the norm that Chinese families would visit relatives, close friends, and neighbours during the first few days of the New Year.

Just like today, it was also quite common to see lion dance performances in and around the town area in the Singapore of the 60s and 70s. However, because the Blue Windows did not house big businesses or organizations, there were hardly any lion dance performances in the neighbourhood during the Chinese New Year period. To make up for this, Father would bring us to Chinatown to watch lion dance performances. These were originally exclusive to the Chinese New Year celebrations, but are now part of any important undertaking, for example, official opening ceremonies, VIP visits, and National Day celebrations. The rattan-framed lion head comes with colourful and attractive features to denote the various moods and strengths of the lion while the performance itself is usually accompanied by loud drumming. Since the dance is acrobatic and requires stamina, lion dance performers are usually able-bodied young men with martial arts skills.

For those Taoists who were also Hokkien, the ninth day of the New Year was a very important day that was to be devoted to the God of Heaven (天公). On that day, or indeed the night prior to that day, our Hokkien neighbours at the Blue Windows would be busy preparing for their prayer session. One prominent worship item that was a must was sugar cane; this practice is still common in Singapore and Malaysia. Apparently, this tradition started many years back when a village in Fujian, South China came under attack on the ninth day of the first lunar month. Before the advancing soldiers entered their village, the villagers hastily escaped to a nearby sugar cane plantation. Hiding deep in the plantation, they desperately prayed to the God of Heaven for their safety. The soldiers did not go near them.

Fire crackers were a must during those early days at the Blue Windows , especially on Chap Goh Mei, the 15th day of the lunar new year. This was known as *Yuanxiao Jie* (元宵节) and is also considered the Chinese Valentine's Day. In olden China, girls and young women, usually confined at home, were allowed to go out on this day in search for their life partners. In Malaysia and less so in Singapore, single women continue to throw mandarin oranges into the sea in hopes of finding a good husband.

The fifteenth day also signified the end of the New Year festivities. According to Grandma, a Teochew saying that marks this day, "chap ngoh kuay, tar poh char boh chey gan quay" (Chinese: 十五过, 男男女女, 找工作): after the fifteenth, all men and women would begin to look for work to do or continue working.

In many ways, how Chinese New Year was celebrated in the 60s and 70s in Singapore is quite different from how it is celebrated now. For one, many celebrations were localized because communication was not as convenient as it is now. The Chinese New Year visits also seem much more personal and meaningful than they are now, when people seem to take one another for granted. Perhaps the convenience of electronic communication has caused these annual visits to lose some of their significance. I am sometimes saddened by the fact that a lot of our cultural heritage has been diluted or lost forever. With firecrackers replaced by a myriad of television programmes and the Internet, much of the simple fun of the old ways of celebration has been lost. Perhaps the significance of traditional festive seasons has been taken for granted in today's increasingly westernised world.

Tomb Sweeping Festival

Another major festival that is celebrated by the Chinese is *Qingming Jie* (清明节, Tomb Sweeping Festival), which usually falls on the first week of the fourth month of the lunar calendar. "Qingming" literally means "clear and bright" and the festival originated during the Tang Dynasty as a means of restricting the numerous, expensive displays that people were devoting to their deceased ancestors to a specific day. Now, the festival remains a period for one to remember and honour one's dead relatives and loved ones. A Chinese poem, written by Du Mu (杜牧), the famous Tang Dynasty scholar/poet, best reflects the sombre mood of the festival. This poem is commonly cited during this festival:

清明时节雨纷纷 (qīng míng shí jié yǔ fēn fēn)
路上行人欲断魂 (lù shàng xíng rén yù duàn hún)
借问酒家何处有 (jiè wèn jiǔ jiā hé chù yǒu)
牧童遥指杏花村 (mù tóng yáo zhǐ xìng huā cūn)

Loosely translated in English:

In the drizzling rain during Qing Ming Festival,
The people on the streets are in deep sorrow.
May I know if there is a tavern nearby?
The cowherd pointed to the Apricot Flower village afar.

This sad poem describes how people had to walk for miles to the cemetery to pay respects to their loved ones. As the festival occurred during the rainy season, the weather complemented the people's fatigue of walking long distances to their ancestors' graves. A traveller longed for a couple of drinks to ease one's thirst, only to be told by a passing cowherd that the nearest tea house was far away in a distant village. This was the sombre mood associated with the festival back then. Nowadays, with modern transportation and the increasing popularity of cremation over burial, the practice of "tomb sweeping", though still relevant, has been very much simplified. Loved ones may just go to the columbarium to pay respects to their deceased relatives without having to sweep a tomb in the literal sense.

In the 1970s, we paid our respects to our great-grand-aunt during Qingming. Her grave was located at the Bukit Brown Cemetery somewhere along Lornie Road. The night before the visit, my mother and grandmother would busy themselves preparing the foodstuff to be used as offerings. Paper money was necessary for the occasion. But instead of the sadness that Du Mu's poem suggests, we were all in good spirits as we considered the trip a kind of family outing.

The next day, Uncle would come and pick us up in his old Morris Minor before dawn. Father, my brothers and I would all squeeze into his tiny car for our excursion to the cemetery. We had to go early as nobody wanted to stand under the hot sun in the later part of the morning. As usual, the first task to execute when we arrived at the cemetery was to find our great-grandaunt's grave, which was quite a large one. Indeed, she must have been quite a well-off woman. However, too many generations had passed between her lives and ours; we did not know much about her except that she migrated to Singapore from Shantou, China, also known as "Swatow".

Despite the size of her grave, finding it was by no means an easy task since all Chinese gravestones looked the same to us. Besides, tall *lalang* and wild grass would have sprouted up in the year since our previous visit, disorientating us by obscuring the footpaths and the words on the gravestones. Once the correct gravestone was located, my father and uncle would proceed with a Taoist prayer ceremony while we children would help with the "tomb sweeping" by clearing the weeds around the grave. It was also customary to place tiny strips of yellow and white paper, joss paper that represented money, on top of the earth covering the grave. My parents told me that this was done to bribe the officials of the netherworld so that our deceased loved ones would have an easier time there.

Meanwhile, there were also other families visiting the graves of their loved ones at the same time, making the cemetery crowded. Moreover, people fired crackers after their prayer sessions during those days. The mood there was anything but sad! Such visits to the cemetery during Qing-ming Festival were quite meaningful since it reminded us to be grateful to our ancestors and to be proud of our roots.

Dragon Boat Festival

Duanwu Jie (端午节, Dragon Boat Festival or Dumpling Festival) is yet another traditional festival that the Chinese continue to celebrate today. The festival falls on the fifth day of the fifth month of the lunar calendar year and commemorates a patriot, Qu Yuan (屈原), who drowned himself in a river when Chu's capital city fell. People rowed their boats out in an attempt to retrieve his body, beating drums at the same time and throwing rice dumplings into the river to scare the fish away and prevent them from eating his body. Dragon boating and rice dumplings are still the key features of the festival today.

On this day, my grandmother and mother would prepare dumplings as offerings to the gods they worshipped and prayed to for good health, good luck and happiness for the family. Back then, rice dumplings were all homemade and were exchanged among neighbours. These *bak chang* (Teochew: 肉粽, meat dumplings) are made by wrapping bamboo leaves around glutinous rice with various other ingredients such as pork, mushroom and small dried shrimps. One kind of *bak chang* had a center made of *tau sar* (Hokkien: 豆沙, sweet bean paste) that was wrapped with a thin layer of pig's intestine. It sounds awful and unhealthy, but most people during those days found the dumpling delicious and worth buying; I am sure this is still true today. My siblings and I always looked forward to this festival as we got to eat the delicious dumplings that Mother made so skillfully. Perhaps the use of fresh ingredients and the more generous use of lard made the dumplings of the olden days seem tastier than what is available nowadays.

Hungry Ghost Festival

When we lived in Queenstown, the seventh month of the lunar year was usually filled with a festive mood as the Chinese celebrated *Zhongyuan Jie* (中元节, Hungry Ghosts Festival), when ghosts and spirits are believed to be free to visit the realm of the living. This day falls on the fifteenth day of the seventh lunar month; it also usually falls around the time Singapore celebrates its National Day on the ninth of August. This festival was taken very seriously by the Chinese and the seventh month remains one of the busier periods for Chinese businessmen such as the incense and paper money makers, the pavilion tents suppliers and installers, and of course, the Chinese restaurants. All over the island, offerings were made to the gods and to the "wandering souls" to ensure peace, good luck, and health for everyone. It was common for a group of people, whether within a business community —

such as group of hawkers in a wet market, small Chinese businesses, or factories — to organize prayer sessions for this festival.

Daily items such as rice, canned food, fruits, and other items, such as cooked chickens and ducks were among the offerings made to these "wandering souls". After a prayer each family member would be given his or her share of the items and this would be followed by a communal dinner in the evening. During that time, it was common for the people to pitch makeshift tents for these dinners. An auction of "hot items" would be carried out at the occasion and the person who bid the highest price for items such as a television set, or even a piece of so-called "Black Gold" (黑金) (a bundle of charcoal wrapped in red paper that had been offered to the gods for good luck and health) would get to bring the item home.

While the auction was going on during the Chinese dinner, wayang or Chinese variety shows would be staged to entertain the guests as well as the unseen spectators: the "wandering souls" or "hungry ghosts". The front rows of the seats in the audience area were left empty for them during the performance. Despite the belief in ghosts and spirits, there was actually nothing eerie about the festival. It was celebrated under bright lights and accompanied by loud music and sounds, with the auctioneer shouting at the top of his voice to attract bidders.

Prior to the television, Chinese opera enthralled people with their colourful costumes. At the Blue Windows, Hungry Ghost Festival entertainment was usually carried out by more than one group at any one time. Concurrently, there might be a wayang show at Mei Ling Street, a Chinese variety show along Margaret Drive, next to the library, and another one near Dawson Road, near my school. Wayang, usually performed in Teochew, Cantonese

A Chinese wayang at Chai Chee estate, 2010. There were no PVC chairs in the 1960s, only wooden ones.

or Hokkien, attracted a lot of people, especially the older generation. During the lunar seventh month, the wayang performances were packed with people from all walks of life. My grandmother and uncle were avid fans but my father, being both busy and English-educated, did not enjoy them as much.

Although the performances were supposed to be staged to please the gods and the "wandering hungry ghosts", the very-much-alive audience definitely enjoyed them too! Wayang, as it is now, was performed by actors and actresses with heavy make-up on the makeshift timber stages with *attap* roof coverings. Traditional Chinese musical instruments such as the *yangqin*, the *erhu* and the drums were commonly included in the opera troupe. Even in those early days, some basic forms of audio systems were available, whether for roadside variety shows or at home. Thus, my electrician uncle was often busy helping the organizers of the temples with all their electrical installation work during such occasions.

Wayang was usually staged in an open space in front of deities or outside temples. Tiong Ghee Temple, the Taoist temple at the top of Mei Ling Hill that Grandma frequented, hosted wayang shows as well. During these occasions, the normally sleepy Boh Beh Kang kampung would be filled with people from near and afar, going up the hill to participate in such festivals. Performances started soon after lunch, with loud Chinese music and dancing to "invite" the gods and hungry ghosts to the shows. This lasted for almost an hour. For some Hokkien operas, modern Mandarin or Hokkien songs were sung by actors and actresses in the early part of the show before the opera began proper. The singers were usually heavily made-up to look like the opera characters but wore modern clothes. In retrospect, it was quite a comical sight, but the people were used to such spectacles.

One of the most famous Teochew opera troupes was *Lau Sai Tor* (Hokkien: 老赛桃, "old race peach"). My other uncle who lived in Penang was a fan of this troupe and he even bought gifts for his favorite opera actors and actresses. Sometimes, opera troupes from Malaysia and even Thailand would perform in our area. In fact, a relative of ours, whom we called Uncle Hua Siang, was an artist who specialized in painting backdrops for the wayang stage. These sceneries depicted famous landscapes in China such as the *Xi Hu* (西湖: West Lake) in Hangzhou, China. Because Uncle Hua Siang travelled with the opera group, he would visit us whenever they came to Singapore. We were very happy to hear him talk about his experiences and adventures in his line of work. Being a friendly and comical person, his presence was always welcome.

Older people, would go to the audience area well before the show started. Grandma was no exception. She would bring a few of us children with her to *chope* (reserve) good viewing positions before they were taken up by other people. We would have to bring our own stools as no seats were provided for the general public; those were meant for the gods and the hungry ghosts. Sometimes, we would bring straw mats and sit on the floor, picnic-style. Grandma would have her favourite straw fan and paper umbrella with her and we would come prepared with titbits such as *kacang putih*.

During those days, it was also very common for enter-prising and daring men to set up gambling or food stalls along the roadside near the makeshift canvas tent that was set up to house the festivities. It seemed as if these stalls mushroomed from out of nowhere just to cater to the large crowd! All these were unlicensed stalls. We had no plastic carriers or containers and had to bring our own cups if we bought sugarcane or coconut juice from the drinks hawkers. Among these temporary hawkers was someone who sold *oh luak* (Teochew: 蚝煎, oyster omelette), another man who sold F&N bottled soft drinks, an Indian man who sold *kacang putih*, and the Satay Man. Despite the occa-sional police raids, it did seem like the authorities closed one eye and let them get on with their activities as much as possible. I suppose the police did not want to disrupt the celebratory mood by conducting frequent crackdowns on these activities. Perhaps they did not want to "offend" the spirits or the "good brothers" (好兄弟)!

Occasional quarrels broke out among the audience. These were usually petty cases of "territorial conflict", or someone blocking another's view. It was indeed very childish but such quarrels were usually minor and were resolved almost immediately. As expected in crowded places in those days, pickpockets and gangsters were constantly on the prowl, but we were not too worried as we had very little for them to take anyway. Besides, our grandmother was our formidable protector.

Though I willingly followed Grandma to those roadside wayang shows, the basic plot of the opera and what was actually happening onstage was a complete blur to me. I was there more for the food and the festive atmosphere. Usually, I would end up pestering Grandma to go home early and she never got to stay till the end of each show!

Towards the later part of the 1970s, roadside Chinese variety shows took over the wayang's function of entertaining the gods and men. Perhaps they wanted to cater to both the demand for more modern performances and the needs of a younger audience. Furthermore, the cost of staging a variety show was also much lower compared to a traditional wayang. For one thing, the performing stage for the *getai* (Chinese: 歌台, Chinese variety show), was smaller and there was no need for the elaborate decoration of the Chinese landscape. The *getai* attracted a lot of people since there was not much alternative entertainment at night. They were usually staged in open-air carparks at the Dawson or Sterling areas up the hill. As with wayang, the music from the stage was loud and clear. Memories of those days are etched deeply in my mind for I was used to doing my homework amidst all the background music from the wayang and *getai*. But no one complained as we considered it a part of our Chinese culture and tradition. Besides, we got to eat a lot of good food during this period!

Double Seventh Festival

On the seventh day of the seventh lunar month, Chinese people celebrate *Qixi* (七夕节, Double Seventh Festival). Legend has it that Niu Lang (牛郎, cowherd), fell deeply in love with a fairy known as Zhi Nu (织女, weaver girl),

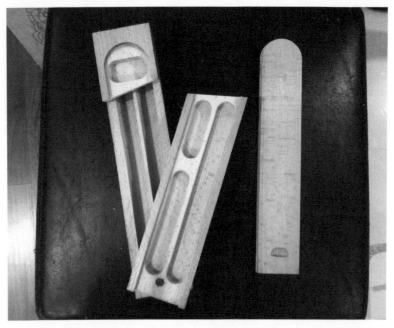

A wooden double-layered pencil box with a sliding cover, very common among students in the 1960s and 1970s.

and married her. As unions between humans and heavenly beings were forbidden, the relationship was doomed from the beginning. Some versions of the story mentioned that she bore him a baby son. The Jade Emperor eventually forced her to return to the heavenly palace, separating the lovers. They were heartbroken. Out of compassion, the Jade Emperor allowed the couple to meet once a year. Each year on the seventh day of the seventh lunar month, a line of magpies fly onto the sky to form a bridge across the Milky Way just so the two lovers can meet for a precious day.

Night prayers to the Weaver Girl normally took the form of offerings of vegetarian foods such as fresh fruit like oranges and pomelos, and goodies like egg cakes and biscuits. As children, we were not concerned with the romantic aspects of the festival. We took part in the celebrations because Grandma told us that we would do well in our studies and find a good life partner in time to come if we prayed to the fairy. So, on this occasion, Grandma would ask Father to give us some extra money — just a few more cents on top of our daily allowance — for us to buy some stationery such as pencils, pencil box, notebooks, etc., that would be blessed during the prayers in the evening.

My favorite item was a small pencil box made of plywood that came with a sliding cover. Unlike most other major festivals, there was no official school holiday for this one. I usually went to the neighbourhood bookshop after school that day to buy my pencil box and offer it as an item for the night prayers. My brothers and sisters had their respective items too. We were pleased to enjoy the festive mood during the evening time when Grandma prepared a makeshift table for the prayers to the fairy. As with all other Chinese customs, paper money and joss sticks were burned during the prayers, which usually lasted till midnight.

Since there were at least three important Chinese festivals to celebrate, the seventh lunar month was a busy time for my parents and Grandma. As the lunar eighth month approached, we looked forward to yet another interesting festival: the Mid-Autumn Festival.

Mid-Autumn Festival

Zhongqiu Jie (中秋节, Mid-Autumn Festival), falls on the fifteenth day of the eighth lunar month and was celebrated by most of my neighbours at the Blue Windows. According to the Chinese legend, one day, ten suns circled the earth at the same time, causing the earth to burn up. Fortunately, an excellent archer by the name of Houyi

(后羿) shot nine suns down, leaving just one sun behind, thus saving the earth from destruction. After performing such a heroic deed, he took Chang'e (嫦娥), a beautiful and intelligent woman as his wife. The version I was told went like this. His rule was cruel and tyrannical; he forced women into serving him as concubines and would kill anyone who opposed him. He also managed to acquire an elixir of life that promised immortality. To prevent the people from suffering under his rule forever, Chang'e secretly drank the elixir and found herself floating to the moon. People, especially young girls, pray to her during the Mid-Autumn Festival to honour her sacrifice and beauty.

Because they are so essential to the celebrations, Mid-Autumn Festival is also called Mooncake or Lantern Festival. Mooncakes were probably first used in prayers to the moon in autumn but our grandmother told us about how Zhu Yuanzhang (朱元璋) used mooncakes in his ploy to overthrow the Yuan dynasty. His men, the rebels, hid secret messages in mooncakes during the Mid-Autumn Festival, which were then distributed to the people. Zhu eventually succeeded in defeating the Mongolians and went on to become the first emperor of the Ming Dynasty.

In my family, the task of buying the mooncakes fell on my uncle. He bought them from Tai Thong Cake Shop (大同饼家), a store in Chinatown that is still in operation today. As children, we waited eagerly for him to bring home boxes of mooncakes. According to Grandma, these mooncakes could only be eaten after they were offered in prayer to Chang'e. Traditional mooncakes are round or square pastries that have a lotus seed paste filling with one or two salted duck egg yolks. During those early days, there were not as many varieties of mooncakes as compared to today. My favourite type of mooncake had a glutinous flour crust and a surface painted with colourful pictures of flowers, the moon, or images of Chang'e and her maids. The crust of this type of mooncake is thin compared to the traditional ones and tasted plain since it had no filling.

For the community at the Blue Windows, Mid-Autumn Festival preparations began a few weeks prior to the actual day. As it is now, mooncakes and lanterns went on sale at the markets and in the streets (there were no shopping centres or supermarkets in Queenstown then). We children always looked forward to receiving small traditional cakes in the shape of piglets placed in plastic baskets. These piglets were actually made of the same batter as that which was used to make mooncakes and were given as free gifts by shops that sold mooncakes. These piglets are still available nowadays but are no longer complimentary.

We bought our lanterns, which came in various shapes, from the provision shop near our house. These caught fire easily as they were made of either coloured cellophane or rice paper. In those days, the estate was dark at night since there was practically no street lighting and this made walking around with lanterns all the more exciting. In the few evenings leading to the actual night of the celebration, adults would escort young children holding lighted lanterns for strolls around the estate. Secondary school-aged children walked around with their lanterns in "gangs", often bringing their younger siblings in tow. Minor scuffles were not uncommon when these "gangs" met: they would throw stones or fire paper bullets from homemade catapults at each other's lanterns for fun, causing them to catch fire.

On the evening itself, most Chinese families would be busy preparing food, especially mooncakes, for prayer to the goddess Chang'e. As always, my grandmother was the one we looked to for instructions. She would prepare the

117

foldable table and fill it up with items such as mooncakes, fruits, mini yams, and water caltrops (a type of water chestnut, uncommon now), not forgetting paper money and joss sticks, all laid out in an orderly fashion. As with Qixi festival, it was customary for children to buy some simple stationery to be used as offerings; in turn, we hoped to do well in our studies. As soon as the prayer session was over, we looked forward to eating the mooncakes. Like today, mooncakes were not cheap back then. Being from a poor family, we could not afford much mooncake but were easily contented and happily ate whatever little portion our parents gave us.

Much of the fun of celebrating both Qixi and Mid-Autumn festival was lost soon after Neil Armstrong landed on moon in 1968. Disenchantment set in when people realized that Chang'e did not, in fact, reside on the moon. Some people thought that paying respects to the moon would be the equivalent to glorifying the Americans and decided to end such practices for political reasons. Although there are still people who still celebrate Mid-Autumn Festival in the traditional way, with the passing of the older generation, the numbers are diminishing.

Christmas

The year-end brought cooler weather, the joy of school holidays, and Christmas and New Year Day celebrations. Unlike modern-day families, most people then — my family included — could not even afford to go to Malaysia for a holiday, much less take an airplane.

Although my family was not Christian, Father's job at Sime Darby, a British firm, meant that we got to cele-brate Christmas. Without fail, the company would hold a Christmas Party for the children of the staff every year.

The water colour painting on the Christmas card that my class-mate, Weng Yew, gave to me in Primary Five. I have framed it up for safekeeping.

We eagerly looked forward to this occasion, which was usually held on the Sunday before the actual Christmas day. I fondly remember the party being held in the function room of the Badminton Hall located somewhere in town. There were magic shows and stage performances, after which Father Christmas would hand out Christmas presents to every child in attendance. The children would queue up and wait for their turn to shake Father Christmas's hand and receive a present. There were also simple refreshments such as cake and soft drinks.

The Christmas party was special for us children since it was one of the very few occasions when we came into contact with an *ang moh* (Hokkien: 红毛, Caucasian). My father's English boss, Mr. Pinder, would dress up as Santa Claus. As children, we were excited at the prospect of shaking hands with this interesting person with the long white beard because his hand was always cold; we did not know that this was simply because he had been sitting in an air-conditioned room all day! However, what occupied us was still the parcel in his other hand. I once received a toy air plane and was so fascinated by it that I told Father that I wanted to be a pilot when I grew up.

Besides the presents for the children, there was also a lucky draw for adults. One year, Father was lucky enough to win the first prize and took home a big Christmas hamper; our delight waned when we realized that most of it consisted of canned food and Western food like ham and butter. Father, however, was very happy that a princely bottle of VSOP was among the items and he saved it for the Chinese New Year.

Being non-Christian, my family did not attend church service on Christmas day and spent the day at home watching programs on our black-and-white television. However, we did send out Christmas greetings. Instead of communicating via text messages or e-cards as we do nowadays, we sent handwritten Christmas cards to our teachers, friends, and loved ones. Not only were these cards beautiful, they were also very personal and meaningful. To this day, I still have a card that my primary school classmate, Weng Yew, handed to me personally. He was very good at art and the card he gave me had a watercolour painting on the front. To this day, that card is worth much more than the tons of electronic cards I now receive as an adult.

Besides the joy of the party and the presents we received, we loved to witness how our few Christian neighbours like my school teacher, Ms. Ho, celebrated the festival. We looked forward in particular to the caroling sessions on Christmas eve, when bus loads of church members would come to the front of her ground floor flat to sing Christmas songs and offer good wishes to the people around. This was especially special since our estate was very quiet at night. The caroling was done in a traditional manner; hymns were sung instead of the more contemporary Christmas "pop" carols that are performed in town these days. There was also hardly any Christmas lighting put up then, yet the joy of Christmas was no less than it is today. Indeed, I cherish the memory of how Christmas was celebrated humbly among residents of the Blue Windows and miss the soothing carols on Christmas Eve and the simple yet beautiful Christmas cards of yesteryear.

A newborn in the family

The birth of a baby at the Blue Windows entailed many traditional, or if you prefer, superstitious practices. These were undertaken regardless of one's professed religion. For instance, once a woman was expecting, the entire family would observe certain rules such as not hammering a nail onto the wall, not painting the house, etc. All these rules had to be strictly adhered to lest the new expectant mother lose her baby or gave birth to a baby with imperfections such as blindness, ugly birth marks or disabilities. It may seem unscientific but there were a surprising number of cases of "defective" babies born because the family had carried out renovation work in the house when the woman was pregnant. Indeed, there was a case in the neighbourhood where a baby was born without an anus, apparently because the family engaged a worker to mend a leaking toilet bowl during the mother's pregnancy. In another case, a baby was born with an unsightly birthmark when the sceptical father went ahead with painting work in their bedroom.

After the birth of a baby, a new mother was expected to adhere strictly to taboos such as avoiding certain foods that were considered harmful. In fact, the new mother was considered "unclean" in the first month after her baby was born. During the confinement, she had to rest at home and be taken care of by a live-in nanny, usually a middle-aged woman who stayed nearby. The new mother also had to consume only specially prepared foods and tonics so that she could recover her health and be able to nurse the baby. According to the older folks, the new mother was also not permitted to wash her hair for one whole month, so as to prevent illness from befalling her in the future. These practices may seem illogical or even unhygienic and superstitious to us now, but were normal in the 1960s and 1970s.

I was told that before the government hospitals were set up, most women gave birth at home with the help of midwives. But during the time when we were in Queenstown, most of the births occurred at the Kandang Kebau (KK) Hospital. I was the first child among my eight siblings to be born in that hospital. My three older siblings were delivered either at home or at a private clinic. In fact, I had the privilege of being brought into this world by a renowned doctor, the late Professor (Dr.) S.S. Ratnam, a medical pioneer and the Head of the Department of Obstetrics and Gynaecology at the former University of Singapore.

The family would hold a traditional celebration to mark the first lunar month after the baby was born. For most Chinese families, offerings were made to gods and deceased ancestors and prayers were carried out at home to bless the newborn child. On this day, red dyed hard-boiled eggs and homemade cakes were distributed to friends and relatives as symbols of life and energy. By then, the name of the baby would have been chosen and sometimes the temple medium would advice that godparents be appointed for the baby.

As far as food for newborns went, there was no such thing as a nutritious milk powder that had a variety of vitamins and supplements. Neither were there specialized shops selling baby products. Instead, we had condensed milk that came in metal cans. Most of the children of that era were fed with "Blue Cross" brand condensed milk. The milk was mixed with water and the solution placed in a glass bottle with a rubber nipple fixed onto the bottle opening. Of course, breast feeding was commonplace in those days. Babies were fed with liquid porridge when they were about six months old.

"Stepping out of the Garden" Ceremony

One of the traditional customs unique to the Teochew community is a coming-of-age ritual known as the "Stepping out of the Garden" Ceremony (出花园仪式). Forget 21 years as the official age when a person is considered an adult. Then, a child would be considered as an adult when he or she reached the age of 15 years. The ceremony fell on the seventh day of the seventh lunar month. In olden-day China, the child was then considered an adult capable of becoming a parent. However, this age was based on the lunar calculation, which is one year ahead of the Western calendar; a child who is 15 under the lunar calendar is legally only 14 years old. Nevertheless, even though that Chinese custom was practised at that time, the law still considered children below 16 minors and child marriage was not common in the 60s or 70s.

What was interesting was the belief that the child needed to be isolated at home on that special day. Firstly, this was to minimize the chances of the child coming into contact with ugly things or people. Teochews believe that the child should come into contact with beautiful things and people as much as possible on that day; if he or she came into contact with ugly things or persons, he or she would also become ugly. This superstition was passed down for generations. To prevent the child from such undesirable encounters, he or she had to stay in a room. Secondly, according to Grandma, it was advisable for other members of the family not to speak to the child unnecessarily because of the belief that the child would require some quiet time to transform him or herself into an adult. Also, they believed that some important gods would be blessing the child on that day and it was not proper for anyone to interfere. Even school teachers knew about this custom then and allowed the child to stay home for the day. A letter from the parent explaining the situation would have sufficed.

When I reached 15 according to the lunar calendar, Grandma and Mother prepared dishes to be offered to ancestors and gods in prayers for good health and good luck; for the whole family in general and for me in particular. Grandma instructed my parents to prepare a feast — in particularly, a whole cooked duck — just for me on that day. The duck, or chicken in other cases, was presented to the child who would then have to gently bite its head. This was a test of courage and signified leadership qualities in anyone who passed it. Of course, I could not consume a whole duck but it was customary to first present it to the child for his or her meal. The leftovers were later eaten by other members of the family. This custom, so prevalent among Teochew families at the Blue Windows then, has long been forgotten and is not commonly practised anymore.

Chinese weddings

Weddings in the late 60s and early 70s were fun, communal events. They were held in makeshift canvas tents pitched on open grounds such as the badminton or basketball courts. My uncle's wedding dinner was held in such a tent at the badminton court in front of our flat. As children, we got

A canvas tent pitched at the badminton court in front of our flat, in preparation for my uncle's wedding dinner.

excited when the tents was set up a day or two before the big event and played under them with the neighbour's children.

On the day of the wedding, the bride and bride-groom would go through the customary Chinese wedding tea ceremony and have photograph sessions during the day. By early evening, friends and relatives would start arriving for the ten-course dinner. The catering restaurant provided cooks who started preparing the food by as early as 4 o'clock in the afternoon. I still remember how the aroma of roasted suckling piglets being prepared would spread to the whole estate. Many of the curious uncles, aunties, and children in the neighbourhood would watch the cooks prepare the food at a side tent. It was preferable that such events occurred on days with good weather, the whole scene got messy and unhygienic if it rained. Fortunately, the weather was fine on my uncle's big day and the dinner went smoothly.

Small Aunt's wedding in December 1968. From left: Father, Mother, the bridegroom, Small Aunt, Big Aunt's daughter, Grandma, Uncle and my younger brother dressed as the page boy.

Towards the end of the dinner, there was always some sort of teasing of the newlyweds. Friends and relatives would come down hard on the bridegroom, demanding that he drink as much as they wanted. The bride was then ushered into the nuptial room, which was rented from one of our neighbours living in the same block. Like today, it was conventional for the couple to make fun of themselves in front of everyone present, all in the spirit of fun. It was also a common practice to collect the leftovers from each table for meals the day after. All of us considered the left-over food delicious and shared them among neighbours, close friends, and relatives. Such was the friendship that we experienced during those good old days in the mid-60s.

Things began to change by the late 1960s and early 1970s when Chinese restaurants became more common.

When Small Aunt got married, the dinner was held at Gay World Park in the Kallang area instead. Without the presence of the makeshift canvas tents, there was less fun and excitement for us children! Nevertheless, we were delighted to attend the Chinese dinner as it was only during big occasions like weddings or Chinese New Year that we children got to eat delicious food.

Malay weddings

During those early years, it felt like racial integration in Singapore was not as common as it is now. Children of different races seldom mixed with each other, at least in my experience. Although my family did not have any close Malay friends, we were able to observe how the Malays lived from the windows of our kitchen and could see the school's staff quarters in the distance across the school field and carpark. As such, we vicariously participated in their Hari Raya celebrations, weddings, and even funerals. I always found their customs interesting as a boy.

At the Blue Windows, I noted that whenever they had a wedding celebration at the quarters, there would likely also be another nearby. This was because the Malay bride and bridegrooms always seemed to live near to one another during those days in kampungs and small estates like the Blue Windows. Instead of driving to fetch the bride on the wedding day, the close proximity meant that the bridegroom could simply walk over to the bride's house with his entourage of relatives and friends. With beautiful flowers tied to bamboo poles, the party would beat their drums and sing along as the wedding procession proceeded to the bride's place. It was an interesting experience and opened my eyes to the richness of Malay culture. Although such practices are still alive today, the atmosphere is entirely different. Then, because of the kampung

Uncle's wedding dinner under a canvas tent at the badminton court. My father is in a tie at the centre of the picture.

spirit, neighbours and friends would gather to witness such wedding processions. Though they retain much of the customs and practices, few Malay wedding processions are carried out in open spaces as was the practice then at the Blue Windows.

Birthday celebrations

Unlike today, birthday celebrations in the 1960s and 70s were normally held for older people above the age of 60 or 65. Children and young adults did not have the special, elaborate birthday celebrations that are so common today. The only birthday ritual that applied to every member of our family was eating a bowl of egg noodles cooked with sweetened water and hard-boiled eggs. No birthday cake, no parties; only the noodles and the egg. And of course, one did not dare expect any birthday present, not even an *angpow*, from anyone, not even your parents. I am sure that well-off families might have had some form of a celebration but most people could not afford that luxury.

It was a different story for the older folks. Their adult children would normally hold a formal dinner for them to commemorate their birthday. When the time came for celebrating Grandma's birthday, my father and my uncle would become cooks. At the same time, the lady folk would make preparations for the dinner that evening, all within the small living room of our flat. Though it was humble, it was perhaps one of the most memorable moments in our lives. For us children, it meant that we would have special food and soft drinks for dinner. This was also the time when our aunties and their children came to visit. For older people like my grandmother, white, peach shaped buns with red tips were a must. The longevity buns were filled with a sweet yam paste and symbolized long life and health. It was only in the mid-70s that "western-style" cakes became a part of our birthday celebrations.

Funerals

My first encounter with the traditional Chinese funeral wake was when one of our close neighbours, a woman in her late sixties we fondly called "Lau Sim" (老婶), died of cancer. Indeed, I still remember Lau Sim as a friendly old woman who was very fond of young children. She was Grandma's best friend and a very good cook who often gave us homemade *kueh nerng kor* and *yutou gao*. Her husband was a retired old man and often came to my house to talk politics with my father and some other neighbours.

A traditional Chinese funeral was held for her. As with all other private events, whether red or white, the funeral wake was held in a canvas pavilion set up at the badminton court. The wake lasted for five days. As children, we felt very scared when we saw the huge hardwood traditional Chinese coffin that required several men to carry. Since her husband, whom we called Lau Chek (老舅), was Teochew, the Taoist rites were performed by their own district association and included chanting and burning incense and paper money. Being close neighbours, my parents were on hand to help the family during their bereavement. As her eldest son worked as a pirate taxi driver, on the actual funeral day, all his *kaki*s [Teochew: 自己, used to refer to friends and family] turned up. Their parked taxis filled up the whole Margaret Drive area, which had very narrow roads. At least 50 taxis followed the hearse during the funeral procession to the cemetery. It was quite a sight!

While death in most cultures is usually regarded as a sad and sober event, the Chinese regard the funeral as a form of celebration if the deceased lived to more than 70 years of age. Some of the funerals involving wealthy elderly persons even had Chinese dance troupe performances at the funeral. This usually involved men and sometimes women dancing with stilts mounted on their legs, and dressed as servants with big heads and paper fans in their hands. Notwithstanding the fact that it was a funeral, the dance was accompanied by Teochew music to create a festive mood. Besides such dances, it was a common practice for the family to invite both Western and Chinese bands to play funeral music during the funeral procession. Such practices remain to this day.

At some funerals, it was not unusual to see the deceased dressed up in multiple layers of traditional Chinese attire for the funeral. In fact, the richer the family of the deceased, the more the layers of clothing the deceased wore. Grandma did not explain the significance of such a practice but I presume that it was to keep the deceased warm and comfortable in his or her final journey to other world, which might be very cold!

A common practice among the well-to-do Chinese Taoist families in the 1960s was paying outsiders and unrelated persons who wished to make some money to "cry" loudly for the deceased during the wake. Such practices, I was told by grandmother, were inherited from the southern province of China, where the rich landlords wanted to give relatives and friends, as well as onlookers, the impression that the deceased was well-loved. This practice, absurd as it seems today, has largely vanished from funerals today.

An elaborate "crossing the bridge" ritual was conducted to "send off" the deceased on his or her final journey to the netherworld. This could last as long as a few hours, from mid-day till midnight. The mourners consisting of immediate family members, children and grandchildren would follow the Taoist priest in walking around the coffin. This was a long process with at least 30 laps around the coffin. In the final lap of the ritual, participants had to walk across a small wooden "bridge"; a metal pail filled with water was placed underneath. This represented the crossing of the river in the netherworld. After crossing the bridge, it was believed that the deceased would lose all his or her memories of this life and enter another realm. The participants would leave the deceased behind and then continue to walk considerably fewer laps around the coffin, which symbolized their return journey into the present world and life.

The order of the line reflected Chinese ideas of hierarchy and status. The men and the boys would go to the front of the line while the women and girls went to the back. Menstruating women were also not permitted to cross the bridge and had to walk by it instead. The "bridge" was in fact a prop about the size of a small coffee table and had two or three steps on each end. When participants were crossing the bridge in the final lap, they would throw coins of different denominations into the pail under the bridge. Symbolically, the coins were used to bribe the officials in the netherworld so that the deceased would have a smoother journey. The coins were either donated to the temple or used to pay for the services of the priests.

During this process, the priest and his assistants, often young boys who were moonlighting, would sing religious songs in Teochew. There was also an accompanying band, usually consisting of middle-aged men, which performed with gongs, trumpets, flutes and other traditional Chinese instruments.

There were a few other funerals in the estate over the years and each one was held at the badminton court. Regardless of whether it was a Taoist or Christian funeral, most of the time, the deceased was buried instead of cremated. However, I recall one particular funeral I attended as a child that involved cremation. My grandmother's aunt had died at a grand old age of nearly 100 years. Being Buddhist, she wanted to be cremated. Unlike the present practice of having the deceased cremated in a state-of-the-art crematorium, hers was an open air cremation that was done at the Bright Hill Monastery (光明山普觉禅寺) near Upper Thomson Road. I witnessed the cremation with my father and my brothers. It took several able-bodied men to carry her wooden coffin and place it in an open-air structure made of bricks, which was filled with rosewood and fragrant woods and leaves. After the Buddhist prayers, her eldest son used a match to light the fire. In just a few minutes, everyone present could make out the skull of the deceased through the burning coffin. While the burning continued, the attendees of the funeral adjoined for a vegetarian meal at the temple. That evening, I was so scared that I had to turn on the light to sleep.

The Chinese belief in the afterlife was stronger then. It was also quite common for people to consult spirit mediums in temples. To the uninitiated, witnessing a

Chinese spirit medium going into a trance and behaving in accordance to the demands of the god being addressed can be a hair-raising experience. At times, the seemingly physically out-of-control Chinese spirit medium might use a sharp long needle to penetrate his chin, allowing blood to drip down. At other times, he might swallow fire by putting a piece of talisman paper with an inscription into his mouth. For the more serious cases, the medium might even make a cut on one of his fingers and use his bloody finger to write out a "prescription" or special message on yellow paper. Most of the time, however, the Chinese medium would simply hand out "prescriptions". These were written in red ink with Chinese brushes on yellow paper. Grandma used these "prescriptions" in two ways. One was to fold the paper into a triangular shape to be used as a "*hu*" (Teochew: short for 护身符子, talisman) for blessing and protection. The other way was to burn the "prescription" over a bowl of plain water and drink the mixture of ashes and water. To the believers, such practices were very effective at solving their problems but an increasing number of young educated people find such practices mere superstition.

A lot of Chinese people believed that the soul of the deceased would make a return trip to the earth to see his or her family members. During the seventh day after the departure of a loved one, family members would make preparations for his or her return by making offerings and burning paper money and items. For Taoists and Buddhists, mourning lasts for the customary period of 49 days. Indeed, there were also many other rituals to be conducted, including a final prayer ceremony that must be carried out a hundred days after the deceased's departure. It was also common practice for the family to engage the services of Chinese mediums to assist them in talking to the deceased, asking him or her questions about the conditions in the other world and requesting the deceased to bless them. Of course these were only practiced by more traditional Taoist families.

The Cantonese funeral wake rituals were significantly different from that of the Teochew or Hokkien. For example, Teochew priests often wore long white coats, while Cantonese priests wore bright yellow gowns and tall head dresses. A dramatic aspect of the Cantonese ritual was when the priest jumped over a pail of burning paper money. With each jump, he would spit out liquid fuel, causing the fire to flash in the pail, chanting the whole time.

It seems like the funeral traditions are one aspect of Chinese culture that has stayed mostly the same. Perhaps this adherence to tradition is performed out of filial piety and a "better safe than sorry" attitude toward death and the afterlife. However, some of the traditions have been simplified or watered down (people used to wear different colours according to their relationship to the deceased but now, all grieving family members simply wear black and white). More elaborate practices are also cumbersome and expensive to perform and are often disregarded. Another change is how fireworks are no longer a fundamental part of the funeral experience.

CHAPTER 6

MEMORABLE EVENTS

A neighbour's eviction

One of my early memories at the Blue Windows is of a family being forcefully evicted from their flat. They stayed on the ground floor of a block of three-storey flats along Dawson Road, near the wet market. My mother and I were on the way to the market in 1961 when we witnessed this family's pitiable situation. There was a group of curious onlookers peeking inside the flat where a middle-aged woman, presumably the mother of the very young children, was crying and pleading with a few officials to let her and the children stay on. But the officials chased them out and left them crying outside what was previously their own flat. As we were not acquainted with the family, we were not sure what followed. I hope they found a place to rest that night.

What occurred before my very eyes was then incomprehensible to me. Later on, my mother explained that the family got evicted because they could not pay the rental arrears. Unfortunately, that incident was not an isolated case and such unpleasant scenes recurred frequently. Nevertheless, that incident instilled in me a strong belief that it was important to have one's own house, a place one could call home.

Flash floods and blackouts

Like now, the monsoon season would bring heavy rain at the end of every year. When it poured continuously for a whole day or so, we could see the water level in the Alexandra canal get higher and higher. Dramatically and inevitably, the canal would overflow and the entire neighbourhood would be flooded. As we were staying on the second storey, my family was not that affected by these flash floods. It was our neighbours who lived on the ground floors who were hit hardest during such heavy rain. Water levels could rise to up to knee level. Each time there was a likelihood of a flash flood, those residents would be busy moving their treasured items, especially their wooden furniture and electrical appliances, to higher ground. Indeed, it was common in those days for them to install raised wooden floors. These acted as a storage area for their belongings during floods.

These floods were both scary and fun for us children. We had a good time during such times, playing with the water. Sometimes, we could even catch some fish that came in from the canal. But those fish were not safe for consumption and were always released. It was also common to see children folding paper boats and releasing them into the drains. The paper boats moving swiftly through the drains right in front of our flat was an interesting sight indeed.

However, unfortunate incidents also occurred during such flash floods. I still remember when the whole neighbourhood was alarmed by the news of a young girl who fell into the canal on a rainy day and was swept away by the strong current. Her body was later recovered a few hundred yards downstream near the Alexandra Road area. It was a sad tale indeed and the incident was the talk of the neighbourhood for many days after. Another time, Lau Gou's son, who was about eight years old, died

The Alexandra Canal was widened in the mid-1970s to prevent flooding. Crescent Girls School (right) remains at the same location.

of a severe infection after sustaining a cut on his leg while swimming in the canal after a downpour. It was indeed a tragedy, given the fact that Lau Gou had passed away just a few weeks before this incident from breast cancer.

As the Chinese proverb goes, misfortunes never come singly (祸不单行) and yet another tragedy was to befall the family within a few months. Compounded by depression and hard work, their father suddenly died of heart failure soon after the death of his youngest son. The family was now left with three boys, who were older, and a girl, who was the youngest, all orphaned at such young ages. We were told that an aunt took them under her wing. My parents and some of our neighbours tried to help them by consoling them and providing them with food and some money. However, there was not much we could do for them in the long term as everyone had their own families to take care of. This must have been one of the most tragic episodes that happened among the people we knew at the Blue Windows.

Another dramatic flooding event occurred during the Hari Raya holiday in 1969. The flood on that day was so severe that it cut off both our water supply and electricity. We ended up having to rely on whatever little water we could get our hands on. Blackouts were just as common as floods during the 60s and 70s. If they occurred at night, the power failure would probably last a few hours and most families had candles and kerosene lamps on standby. Fortunately, like most families during those early days, we did not have the luxury of air-conditioning. This meant that we still got to bed as usual in the event of a blackout. The fact that our windows were always open actually meant we could even sleep better in the complete darkness that a blackout entailed! Although these incidents were inconvenient, the people at the Blue Windows seemed to have accepted the occasional blackout as a part and parcel of life. In fact, these were eventful moments in our lives as children.

The Bukit Ho Swee fire

During the Hari Raya Haji holiday on the 25 May 1961, the whole estate was shocked to learn about a big fire that occurred at the Bukit Ho Swee area along Tiong Bahru and Havelock Road. The entire area was totally destroyed in a short span of time. Fortunately, those who stayed at the Blue Windows were not affected since the fire occurred at a distance from the Margaret Drive area. In total, four people were killed and approximately 16 000 were rendered homeless.

All our neighbours were concerned about the fire, which naturally became the talk of the town for a few weeks. As a young boy then, I was not sure about what was going on. I only remember my father saying that we all needed to be more aware of the dangers of fire. This vigilance was an extension of his personality; even before sitting down on a bench next to a tree, Father would survey his surroundings just in case anything fell on him or his loved ones.

The fire eventually impacted the Blue Windows indirectly. Very soon, some of the previous Bukit Ho Swee residents began moving into our estate. Another consequence of the fire was that the Housing and Development Board (HDB) kicked off a mass housing programme for the displaced residents. The new statutory board later inaugurated a home ownership scheme in which citizens could use their Central Provident Fund (CPF) to purchase their flats.

Chinese School Students' demonstration

Another significant event that occurred in 1961 was an examination boycott by Chinese school students. They were protesting major changes made by the Ministry of Education to the Chinese secondary school education system. The students picketed the year-end examination centres to boycott the Chinese Secondary Four examination, causing it to be delayed by an hour. According to news reports, the student boycotters initially acted peaceably and simply tried to persuade their fellow students against taking the examination. However, the atmosphere turned aggressive when some picketing students began booing and insulting candidates who entered or left the examination centre. This was at the MOE building along Tanglin Road, which was at one end of Margaret Drive. The situation got worse when some students formed a human chain to prevent other candidates from getting into the examination centre. When the situation became more serious, policemen (then still under the British Government and attired in beige khaki shorts and short-sleeved, light blue shirts) were called in and arrests were made. The building was not far away from our flat and residents could sense the tense situation. Police car sirens were heard passing by our flats and all residents were told to stay indoors.

It was only when I reached secondary school that I understood the severity of the conflict that I witnessed. According to Father, the students wanted to hinder the government's proposal to change the education system from the 3-3 system to a 4-2 system. The 3-3 system refers to the system that Chinese schools followed: three years of secondary school education followed by another three years of pre-university education. In a bid to create a truly national education system, the Ministry of Education wanted to make the English-stream schools' system of four years of secondary school education followed by another two years of pre-university education apply to the Chinese schools as well.

While I was blissfully ignorant, my father was decidedly worried and repeatedly cautioned Small Aunt, who was enrolled in a Chinese-medium secondary school then, against getting involved in politics. She used to bring her schoolmates to our house after school on the pretext of discussing their homework. What they actually did was exchange ideas on the political issues of the day. During weekends, her small group of schoolmates, both girls and guys, would even have dinner at our house. My mother was initially quite happy to prepare meals for them. After some time however, the fact that we were not well-to-do meant that she had to tell my aunt and her friends to go somewhere else for dinner. Fortunately, Small Aunt did not get herself into trouble and managed to pass her examinations. Small Aunt eventually left her pre-university class and became a private Chinese tutor.

Racial riots

If the student unrest that occurred in 1961 were anxiety-ridden times for residents at the Blue Windows, the nationwide racial riots and the bomb blasts in 1964 were even more worrying. My father returned home from his office at Robinson Road one evening, telling us to stay indoors as riots between the Malay and Chinese had started downtown. At least no persons were harmed during the student unrest since the students' resistance was more political than physical. Innocent lives, however, were lost as a result of the racial riots.

Father even told us that he saw blood splattered on the street when he was on his way home. A homemade bomb had been detonated along the road. The island-wide situation then was tense and urgent. Regardless of race or age, most people were very worried about the uncertainties as a result of the racial unrest in Singapore. Another incident occurred in 1965 when a bomb exploded at MacDonald House. Years later, I read that these bomb blasts were carried out by saboteurs from Indonesia, who opposed the Federation of Malaysia, which they saw as a threat. Apparently, this was part of an Indonesian policy called *Konfrontasi*.

Such social and political crises affected not only the adults, but also schoolchildren like me. One time, our school headmaster told us that each student had to bring some canned food to school in case the government imposed curfews and we were required to stay in school for a few days. In response, my mother armed my younger brother, younger sister and me with a can of sardine fish and a packet of dried egg noodle each (we did not have instant noodles in those days). We did not contribute much as my parents had eight children to feed. However, my form teacher was very understanding and did not impose a minimum amount of food for her students to bring to school. Fortunately, none of these items had to be used and were eventually returned to us.

Despite the overall tension in Singapore, the mood at the Blue Windows then was one of cautious curiosity rather than fear. For one thing, most of the residents at the estate were Chinese, with only a few Indian families. Our immediate Malay neighbours were the gardeners and school attendants working for the primary schools behind our flat, and they were very friendly and helpful. Fortunately for us, life went on as usual despite the ugly riots and the occasional explosion that occurred downtown.

One thing that was interesting was how the Peranakan Chinese, who are neither strictly Chinese nor Malay, were put in difficult situation during the racial riots. Most of them looked and spoke Malay but also retained certain Chinese cultural practices. Obviously, there was a risk of them being attacked by both Chinese and Malay rioters. Father told us that this was exactly what happened to one of his colleagues, a Peranakan Chinese man who also stayed at the Blue Windows. At the peak of the racial crisis, this man was returning home from work late one evening. He was approached by a group of Chinese youth on the way to the bus station. They asked him what his race was. With his brownish complexion, he tried to convince them that he was Chinese. Unfortunately for him, he could not speak much Hokkien or Mandarin. In the end, he was beaten up simply for looking Malay. Fortunately, his injuries were not that serious and he managed to amble along.

But before he could even get to the bus station, a few Malay guys, convinced that he was Chinese, started shouting at him. In distress and pain, the poor man quickly explained in fluent Malay that he was in fact Peranakan.

Student activists at Nanyang University

Student unrest occurred in the same year at the then Nanyang University in Jurong and in some Chinese medium schools, notably the Chinese High School in Bukit Timah. The government at that time was very worried about universities being used as training grounds for Communist cadres and a total of 51 arrests were made for alleged communist-related activities. These were mostly student leaders or individuals who were active in the Student Union.

Brother Hong was the eldest son of my father's cousin, who owned the toy shop at Golden Hill. He was a student at the then Nanyang University and had been arrested by the police. Brother Hong's arrest naturally caused much worry for his immediate family. My father, being part of the extended family, advised his cousin on how to handle the matter. In any case, we were told that he was eventually expelled from Nanyang University but was not jailed. At least Father's cousin's second son was English-educated at the University of Singapore and managed to stay out of trouble.

CHAPTER 7

A NEW QUEENSTOWN

Rumours of redevelopment

Late one particularly quiet evening in 1971, Father returned home from an informal meeting with some of the neighbours. His expression was one of disappointment and he calmly announced that we would have to vacate our flat and find a new place to live. A discussion between my parents ensued. Mother, reassuring and calm as always, said that the children were growing up anyway, it was time to move. We would make do with whatever we had.

We children were very sad to hear the news as we had grown to love the place and people at the Blue Windows. In fact, some of our neighbours had already received official letters from the government stating that they had to vacate their flats as the area had been selected for redevelopment. The government would help them find alternative housing. At that point, we had yet to receive such a letter and were still hoping that it would never come.

Even a few years prior to 1971, there were already rumours that the government intended to redevelop the entire estate. The main reason was because some of the flats built in the early 1960s were showing signs of instability. One of the worst-hit blocks must have been the one in which our neighbours, the Yeo family, resided. It was a four-storey block just next to the canal and it was obvious just from looking at it that the block was leaning slightly to one side. It was certainly a sight that caused much worry for all the occupants of the block as well as their neighbours. The situation in Mr. Yeo's flat was serious — water that was spilt on the dining table would flow towards one side of the table. Most neighbours believed that the cause of the leaning was the soil structure since the block was next to soft clay by the side of the canal that frequently flooded over during prolonged and heavy downpour. Till now, none of us really know the reasons for the poor foundations of the buildings.

A more modern lifestyle

By the early 1970s, our way of life had changed rapidly on various fronts. The Hock Lee bus services were gone by then, taking with it the No. 9 bus that brought Mother and us to Chinatown's Majestic Theatre and the No. 3 bus that I used to take to my secondary school along Kim Seng Road. In their place were new buses from the Singapore Bus Services (SBS). Pirate taxis also disappeared from our roads and were replaced by black-body, yellow-top taxis with licensed taxi drivers and fare meters. With the departure of the pirate taxi, commuters no longer had to go through the frustration of bargaining with drivers over the fare.

Even the physical landscape surrounding our estate started to change. High-rise HDB flats started to appear in the Mei Ling Heights area, the area that special memories for us and was the site of many activities, particularly during Chinese festivals such as the Seventh Month and the Chinese New Year. The wooden-structured Tiong Ghee temple that Grandma used to worship at, then located on the small hill, was demolished in 1968. It was later rebuilt as a concrete and brick temple in 1973 at its current location at Stirling Road. From behind our kitchen windows, an open school field was replaced with a block of sixteen-storey HDB flats.

On the home front, changes came fast and furious. One indication of the pace of change was the improvement of our household appliances. Prominent among these advances must be the advent of the television. Increasing affluence also meant that more and more people were replacing their black-and-white television sets with coloured ones. Of course, by then, Rediffusion services were getting less popular. Most of the black-and-white coloured rotary telephones had also been replaced by colour-tone push button telephone.

Things were moving fast. Most people were too preoccupied with their desire for material upgrades to realize the effects of such rapid change. For better or for worse, the simplicity disappeared and life at the Blue Windows changed.

Changing family circumstances

While work life in the early 1970s was not as frentic as it is today, people who worked as employees had their fair share of stress and grievances. Father, whose work at Sime Darby involved handling large sums of money as a cashier, was no exception. As an experienced but low ranking staff, Father earned a rather small salary and often had to work overtime to support our large family. As a father myself, I know what a burden it must have been for my father to take care of so many children. Despite having to work long hours, and pay the rent and other household bills, my father did not complain at all. Instead, he worked hard and took on part-time jobs to sustain the family.

One evening in the later part of 1972, Father returned from work in the evening and told my mother that he was experiencing a lot of stress in the office. He told her that his company was facing some internal problems. At that time, I could not fathom what they were discussing or how serious it was. I only knew that Father had to answer a lot of questions regarding financial matters from his many bosses and was very tired and stressed out. Years later, the local newspaper stated that his big boss, whom we as children knew as the "Father Christmas" during the company's Christmas Day celebrations, had been dismissed as the Director of Sime Darby. He was convicted of committing white-collar crime when he was heading the company. His arrest resulted in the internal restructuring of the company.

In his relatively junior position as the cashier, Father was not directly affected by the incident or the government investigation. Nonetheless, he was apprehensive and retired from work soon after the incident at the age of 55. He passed away three years later when I was at university. His passing was a severe blow to our family as most of us, except my two older brothers who just started working, were still schooling. Nevertheless, Father left behind a legacy of his own for his children — we learnt the value of honesty, gentle manners, and being respectful in dealing with all people, regardless of their social status or background.

Moving house

The year was 1973. The final curtain finally fell on the Blue Windows, taking away the old ways of life in our little estate. The notice for us to vacate our Margaret Drive flat finally arrived at our doorstep. Unwillingly, our family made preparations to move. Visits among neighbours came to a somewhat abrupt halt as everyone got busy packing and preparing to leave. We were no different.

We moved out in March. Luckily, moving out of the flat was not that difficult since we had the help of our electrician uncle and a few of his able-bodied workers. Come to think of it, the actual act of moving house was quite comical. My uncle drove his company lorry to the front of the flat on the side of the balcony. Instead of moving all our furniture and household items through the staircase, his workers threw the items out of our second-storey flat, to their colleagues at the ground floor or right into the lorry. Our belongings were loaded into the lorry in double-time and moved three kilometers to our new flat.

The next day, when I went to school, my classmate who lived opposite my flat at the Blue Windows came up to me with an amused expression. He told me that he had witnessed my family's "innovative" method of moving house the day before and went around telling our friends about it during morning assembly.

Tiong Bahru

Our new place was a rental flat that was actually older than our home at the Blue Windows. The new flat was on the third storey of a four-storey flat facing Tiong Bahru Road. At least it was nearer to the city, we thought, especially Chinatown. There was also an excellent food center opposite us. Unfortunately, in my mind, the area did not live up to the serene yet dynamic landscape of the Blue Windows. We ended up in a unit that was right in front of the bus stop and next to the busy, noisy and dusty main road. From then on, I developed a strong aversion to noise and loud sounds; I became an acoustic consultant specialising in noise control later on. We had no choice but to adapt to this new environment; it was especially tough on my aged Grandma.

I was walking home on a cool and wet evening in December 1973 when something caught my eye at the hawker centre along Tiong Bahru Road. A thin and frail old woman was sitting by herself next to a stall selling noodles. She was holding a green waxed paper umbrella in one hand and resting the other on the table. It dawned on me that this lonesome figure was in fact my grandmother. I was surprised since Grandma seldom ventured out of the new flat, even months after we moved in, without my aunt or mother. She was delighted to see me and, with a sad and quiet smile, invited me to join her.

I had just had dinner at my classmate's house after revising our work together and politely declined her offer of a bowl of fishball noodles. Instead, I ordered a glass of sugarcane juice and sat with her for our last meal alone. We waited for her noodles quietly; there was not much to say, maybe due to the generation gap. It was rare that I got to eat with Grandma alone, especially when I had so many siblings. We usually ate at home with my immediate family, or at restaurants with the whole extended family.

The forlornness in Grandma's eyes was discernible. It was obvious to me that she had been trying hard to adjust to the new environment at Tiong Bahru; on top of the unfamiliar faces were the unfamiliar languages. A true-blue Teochew from Swatow, she could only understand Teochew. Most of our new neighbours were Cantonese, it must have been isolating, to say the least. After all, she used to spend all her spare time chit-chatting with neighbours when we were at the Blue Windows. After staying there for more than a decade, she had established firm friendships with the neighbours there. At Tiong Bahru, other than her family, she had no one else to talk to.

At the end of the dinner, I offered to pay for her 30 cent meal with the little money I had, but Grandma insisted on paying. I gave in. It was drizzling slightly when we walked home. Calmly, she told me that she knew that she was getting older. "I'm sure I won't be able to see you graduate from university", she sighed, "but remember, *ah shun* [Teochew: 阿孙, grandson]: good people will always take the good road, for goodness begets goodness in turn". I was going to get enlisted into National Service soon and she told me to take care of myself and serve the nation well. Silently, I nodded. At that moment, I wished that we could have somehow gone back in time, to a time when Grandma sat with us children on a straw mat on the badminton court in front of our previous flat. Somehow, I found myself holding onto her arm as we made our way home. Together, we navigated the unfamiliar landscape of Tiong Bahru and got home.

Grandma went to stay with my uncle in a row of pre-war shop houses at Boat Quay a few months after that evening. Another few months passed and we got news that she passed away in her sleep. I felt loss and confusion, but for some reason sadness eluded me. Perhaps I felt that Grandma had simply moved on to her next journey, and I knew that she would take a good road. Although I wish our last dinner and walk together was at our beloved Blue Windows, but I still treasure those last moments I had with her.

AFTERWORD

The older low-rise flats at Duchess Estate contrast starkly with the more recent high-rise developments.

It has been almost four decades since my family and I moved out of the Blue Windows. They say time flies and I have come to agree with this. I've stayed in various areas in Singapore since but none of these places can inspire the same sense of nostalgia that I feel for the Blue Windows. For most people of my generation, the "good old days" are dead and gone, and will only remain as sweet memories.

In a recent visit back to Queenstown, I drove along the now almost unrecognizable Margaret Drive. I felt conflicted by the new but congested developments that

were taking place there. The once familiar landscape no longer existed. It was indeed painful to realize that many of the old Queenstown landmarks were gone, including the low-rise SIT flats with the blue louvre glass windows. Yet the new, imposing HDB flats, with their huge glass panes and beautifully designed facades amazed me. A sense of remorse overcame me: a part of our national heritage and our rich past had been eliminated in the endless pursuit for a more modern lifestyle.

The scarcity of land in Singapore makes it understandable: urban planners need to get rid of the old to make way for the new. Is it possible to be more selective and cautious when deciding what should be torn down and what should be preserved? Not all these structures may be high-profile but they may possess value in terms of their unique architecture or historical significance. A case in point would be Forfar House, regarded as one of the earliest high-rise public flats in Singapore. Yet every time I visit Queenstown, I realize a chunk of it has disappeared.

153

I've stayed in various areas in Singapore since but none of these places can inspire the same sense of nostalgia that I feel for the Blue Windows. The seminary of the Queenstown Baptist Church, which was still standing in 2011 was gone when I drove by one year later. The Tah Chung Emporium, the Queenstown Remand Prison and most of the low-rise flats have all disappeared. The two cinemas and the hawker centre cum wet market have been converted into churches and upgraded respectively.

Some remnants remain: the Church of the Good Shepherd, a single-storey pitched roof building; Masjid Jamae, the mosque at the junction of Margaret Drive and Tanglin Road; the Tiong Ghee Temple, albeit with an upgraded building and façade. Princess House, aged no doubt, still stands and was gazetted in 2007 for conservation. The Queenstown Branch Library is still operating, with a healthy number of student and adult visitors. In fact, not that much has changed since its glory days as the first public library in the heartlands of Singapore.

Still, I sometimes wonder if there will be any landscapes familiar to my generation that future generations will be able to come into actual contact with. The Queenstown of my childhood is gone and a new dwelling enclave has emerged in its place. It is now up to the next generation to treasure their living space. As for me and those who once stayed at Queenstown, the Blue Windows lives on, if not in our hearts, then at least between the covers of this book.

MAP OF QUEENSTOWN IN THE 1960S AND 1970S

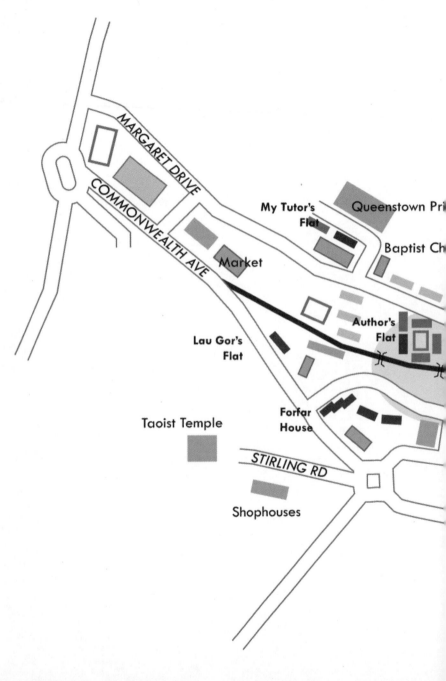

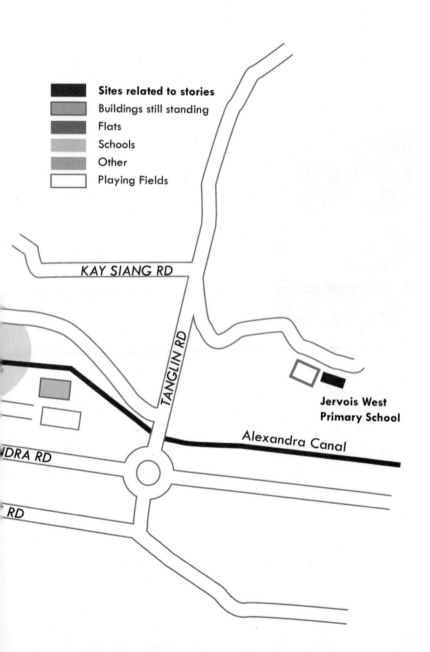

Sites related to stories
Buildings still standing
Flats
Schools
Other
Playing Fields

KAY SIANG RD

TANGLIN RD

Jervois West
Primary School

Alexandra Canal

NDRA RD

RD

ABOUT THE AUTHOR

Tan Kok Yang spent his formative years in Queenstown in the 1960s to 1970s. He attended Kim Seng Technical School and Queenstown Secondary Technical School in the 1970s. In 1980, he graduated with a Degree in Building from the University of Singapore and went on to obtain a Masters Degree in Building Science (Acoustics Major) in 1988 from the National University of Singapore. He also holds a Doctorate (1997) in Housing and Environmental Studies from the University of New England, N.S.W. Australia. A former lecturer in Environmental Science at the Singapore Polytechnic, he now runs his own acoustic consultancy firm. His interests in environmental issues, in particular, that which affect human habitation, prompted him to write about life of the people who once lived in Queenstown.

2013